AQA English Literature A:
Literature of World War One

AS

Exclusively endorsed by AQA

Stella Canwell

Nelson Thornes

Published in 2008 by:
Nelson Thornes Ltd
Delta Place
27 Bath Road
CHELTENHAM
GL53 7TH
United Kingdom

08 09 10 11 12 / 10 9 8 7 6 5 4 3 2 1

A catalogue record for this book is available from the British Library

ISBN 978 0 7487 8294 9

Cover photograph by Photolibrary

Page make-up by Pantek Arts Ltd, Maidstone, Kent

Printed and bound in Great Britain by Scotprint

Every effort has been made to trace the copyright holders but if any have been inadvertently
overloooked the publishers will be pleased to make the necessary arrangement at the first
opportunity.

Contents

Acknowledgements

The author and publishers wish to thank the following for permission to use copyright material:

The Assessment and Qualifications Alliance for the assessment objectives for English Literature A from the GCE specimen mark scheme; Patrick Aylmer for extracts from Mary Borden, *The Forbidden Zone*, Heinemann (1929), Hesperus Press forthcoming; Faber and Faber Ltd for extracts from Frank McGuiness, *Observe the Sons of Ulster Marching Towards the Somme* (1986); and Sean O'Casey, *The Silver Tassie* from *Plays* by Sean O'Casey (1998) Act I, pp.186-7, Act 4, pp. 250-2; Samuel French Ltd on behalf of the author's estate for extracts from Miles Malleson, *Black 'Ell* (1916); David Higham Associates on behalf of the author for Herbert Read, 'To A Conscript of 1940' from *Selected Poetry* by Herbert Read; Barbara Levy Literary Agency on behalf of the Estate of George Sassoon for Siegfried Sassoon, 'A Working Party'; Peter Newbolt for Sir Henry Newbolt, 'Vitai Lampada'; W W Norton & Company, Inc for Rita Dove, 'Alfonzo Prepares to Go Over the Top' from *American Smooth* by Rita Dove. Copyright © 2004 by Rita Dove; Oxford University Press for an extract from Peter Fussell, *Great War and Modern Memory* (1975); Penguin Books Ltd for extracts from Henri Barbusse, *Under Fire*, trs. Robin Buss, Penguin Classics (2003). Translation copyright © Robin Buss 2003. Introduction copyright © Jay Winter 2003; and extracts from 'Blackadder Goes Forth' from *Blackadder: The Whole Damn Dynasty*, Michael Joseph (1998). Copyright © Richard Curtis and Ben Alton 1989; PFD on behalf of the author for an extract from Edmund Blunden, *Undertones of War*. Copyright © Edmund Blunden; Random House Group Ltd for an extract from Adam Thorpe, *Nineteen Twenty-One*, Jonathan Cape; and Erich Maria Remarque, *All Quiet on the Western Front*, Jonathan Cape/Vintage; Diana Raymond for an extract from Ernest Raymond, *Tell England*; James Slater for May Cannan, 'Perfect Epilogue' from *The Tears of War* by May Canaan and Basil Quiller Couch, Cavalier Paperbacks (2000); Tate Images for an extract from a letter by Paul Nash from *Outline: An Autobiography* by Paul Nash, Columbus Books (1988) by Paul Nash. Copyright © Tate, London 2007; Rosemary Vallender for an extract from Helen Thomas, *World Without End*; A P Watt Ltd on behalf of the Literary Executors of the Estate of the author for an extract from H G Wells, *Mr Britling Sees It Through*; Every effort has been made to trace the copyright holders but if any have been inadvertently overlooked the publishers will be pleased to make the necessary arrangement at the first opportunity.

Photo credits:
pp22,38,39:Imperial War Museum; pp28,34,51:Bettmann/CORBIS; p29: Tony Larkin/Rex Features; p.30 NOT ABOUT HEROES Performed at the Barons Court Theatre 2005,directed by Ian Flintoff. Siegfried Sassoon (Dov Citron) and Wilfred Owen (Martin Scully). Image Courtesy of MAD House Plays www.madhouseplays.com; p35:Getty Images/Hulton Archive; p37:Michael Nicholson/CORBIS; p45:Stapleton Collection/Corbis; p56: CORBIS; p60:Hulton-Deutsch Collection/CORBIS; p70:Haywood Magee/ Stringer Hulton Archive Getty Images; pp74,83:Robbie Jack/CORBIS; p76: Tristram Kenton/Lebrecht Music; p80:Rex Features; pp88,89,90:Hulton-Deutsch Collection/CORBIS; p91:Picture Post/Stringer Getty Images

Introduction

Nelson Thornes and AQA

Nelson Thornes has worked in collaboration with AQA to ensure that this book offers you the best support for your AS or A Level course and helps you to prepare for your exams. The partnership means that you can be confident that the range of learning, teaching and assessment practice materials has been checked by the senior examining team at AQA before formal approval, and is closely matched to the requirements of your specification.

Blended learning

Printed and electronic resources are blended: this means that links between topics and activities between the book and the electronic resources help you to work in the way that best suits you, and enable extra support to be provided online. For example, you can test yourself online and feedback from the test will direct you back to the relevant parts of the book.

Electronic resources are available in a simple-to-use online platform called Nelson Thornes learning space. If your school or college has a licence to use the service, you will be given a password through which you can access the materials through any internet connection.

Icons in this book indicate where there is material online related to that topic. The following icons are used:

Learning activity

These resources include a variety of interactive and non-interactive activities to support your learning.

Progress tracking

These resources include a variety of tests that you can use to check your knowledge on particular topics (Test yourself) and a range of resources that enable you to analyse and understand examination questions (On your marks…).

Research support

These resources include WebQuests, in which you are assigned a task and provided with a range of web links to use as source material for research.

Study skills

These resources support you develop a skill that is key for your course, for example planning essays.

Analysis tool

These resources help you to analyse key texts and images by providing questions and prompts to focus your response.

When you see an icon, go to Nelson Thornes learning space at www.nelsonthornes.com/aqagce, enter your access details and select your course. The materials are arranged in the same order as the topics in the book, so you can easily find the resources you need.

How to use this book

This book covers the specification for your course and is arranged in a sequence approved by AQA. The book is divided into eight chapters, beginning, In Chapter 1 with an introduction to the English Literature A Specification and how you will be assessed. Chapter 2 explains your coursework task and texts. Chapters 4 to 6 each provide guidance on your wider reading in the genres of poetry, prose and drama. Chapter 7 helps to get you familiar with the context question, taking you through examples of the type of extracts you might be expected to deal with in the examination. Finally, Chapter 8 takes you through an examination paper, demonstrating how to tackle the paper and focus your answer using key words.

Learning objectives

At the beginning of each section you will find a list of learning objectives that contain targets linked to the requirements of the specification.

The features in this book include:

Key terms

Terms that you will need to be able to define and understand. These terms are coloured blue in the book and their definition will also appear in the Glossary at the back of this book.

Did you know?

Interesting facts to extend your background knowledge.

Links

Links to refer you to other areas of the book which cover the topics you are reading about.

Further reading

Suggestions for other texts that will help you in your study and preparation for assessment in English Literature.

Activity

Activities which develop the skills you will need for success in your English Literature course.

Questions

Questions which help to focus your reading of key extracts and prepare you for writing on extracts in the exam and in your coursework.

 Examination-style questions

Questions in the style that you can expect in your exam. You will find these in Chapter 8.

Summary

A summary of what is covered in this chapter of the book.

AQA examination questions are reproduced by permission of the Assessment and Qualifications Alliance.

1 Introduction

This book has been written to help you to be as successful as possible in your AS AQA English Literature A course. It will introduce you to the relevant **subject matter** that you need to **know and understand**, as well as the **skills** you need to develop and apply in order to read, analyse, interpret and write about your texts.

In this chapter we are going to look at:

- the kinds of reading you will be undertaking
- the wider reading list
- the assessment objectives
- the assessment grid.

This book will give you help, support and advice on how to:

- approach your set texts
- succeed with your coursework
- tackle wider reading in prose, poetry and drama
- select wider reading in non-fiction
- approach a sample examination paper.

Your AS English Literature course

This is one of three AS textbooks for AQA English Literature A, one each for the three optional areas of study. Your chosen option is the literature of World War One, which is the focus for this book and all your reading for the AS course. You will be studying **one poetry** text for the written examination, and **one prose** text and **one drama** text for your coursework.

You will also need to read widely in the literature from and about World War One. Your wider reading will probably include some whole texts, but will no doubt also include a good many extracts. Reading the extracts will help you to appreciate the variety and range of the literature of World War One, covering writers of both **genders** as well as texts of all **genres**.

Your teacher will establish the foundation and framework for your reading, but, as you progress through your AS course, and once you gain confidence and experience as a reader, **you** should increasingly be the one who chooses and explores aspects of the literature. You will then be in a position to be able to pursue your own interests, tracing connections, comparisons and contrasts between texts in the **shared context** of World War One literature. Your study of the chosen area of literature will therefore consist of both **close and wide reading**.

How to become an informed, independent reader

Before we start to explore your chosen area of literature, we are going to establish what kind of reader you need to be. The aim of AS English Literature is to enable you to develop as an informed, independent reader and confident critic of literary texts.

As an informed, independent reader, you will learn to build a reading of a text through:

■ careful and close reading that provides you with appropriate and
specific evidence to support your interpretation

■ consideration and understanding of other possible readings

■ research into the contexts of both reading and writing.

The AQA English Literature A Specification provides you, the reader,
with maximum opportunities for both writing coursework and sitting an
open-text examination (an examination where you are allowed to take a
copy of your set text into the examination and are encouraged to use it to
help answer the questions). Such opportunities encourage research on the
one hand and close focus on specific parts of texts on the other.

Reading for meaning

As you read the literature of your chosen period, you will need to be
actively engaged with your texts in order to develop **informed, personal
responses**.

The AQA English Literature course is built on a philosophy of reading
and meaning which it is important that you understand and share.

We think that:

Reading

■ is an active process: the reader is an **active creator**, not a passive
recipient of second-hand opinion – *you are the 'maker of meaning'*

■ can never be 'innocent': all readings are historically, socially and
individually specific – *you bring your own personal context and
experience to the text*

■ is not a single skill: some kinds of reading are more demanding than
others – *think, for example, of the comparable difficulty of reading a
Mills and Boon romance on the one hand, and a Jane Austen novel on
the other*

Meaning

■ for an individual reader, depends as much on what is brought to the
text as on what is contained within it – *your own experience will
influence the way you read the text*

■ will not necessarily be instantly accessible – *you may well need to
research difficult or obscure references and vocabulary, for example,
before you can tease out meaning*

■ will be different on different occasions, and changeable as a result of
discussion and reflection – *when you re-read a text, for example, you
may find your response is different from your first reading; discussion
with your peers and/or your teacher or reading a critical commentary
may also influence and change your response to a text*

■ can be multiple; different readings of a text can co-exist – *you need
to be aware that some texts are ambiguous or capable of delivering
multiple meanings and it is your own selection of and response
to textual evidence which will determine your own personal
interpretation.*

Wider reading for your AS English Literature course

Your AS course, then, is a coherent collection of reading in the literature
of World War One. The texts for detailed study (the novel and play
in your coursework and the set poetry text in the examination) are
supported by your wider reading which provides the context.

The purpose of your wider reading is to:

- provide you with the opportunity to discover and explore your own interests and enjoyment, developing your awareness of the ways you respond to and understand different kinds of writing
- enable you to consider the **typicality** or **shared context** of your reading so that you can explore connections, comparisons and contrasts
- encourage you to see different points of view, exploring the ways that different writers describe a similar experience or situation
- enable you to discover and understand the ways different writers choose to communicate with you, the reader, exploring choices of form, structure and language.

The specification for the AQA AS English Literature A course provides you with a reading list from which you and your teachers can choose whole texts and extracts for study. It covers all relevant **genres**, writing by both **male and female** authors, significant and influential **literature in translation**, as well as **non-fiction** texts. The following is the Wider Reading List.

Texts for AS – World War One

* denotes post-1990

Choose three texts (or the equivalent in extracts) of any genre.

Prose fiction

Any of the ten named texts for Unit 2, plus

*Ben Elton, *The First Casualty* (Bantam, 2005)

Ernest Hemingway, *A Farewell to Arms* (1929)

Ford Madox Ford, *Parade's End* (1924–8)

Irene Rathbone, *We That Were Young* (1932)

*Adam Thorpe, *Nineteen-Twenty-One* (Vintage, 2001)

Virginia Woolf, *Jacob's Room* (1922)

Prose non-fiction

Memoirs

Edmund Blunden, *Undertones of War* (Penguin, 1928)

Vera Brittain, *Testament of Youth* (Virago, 1933)

Robert Graves, *Goodbye to All That* (Penguin, 1929)

History and testimony

William Thomas Allison and John Fairley, *The Monocled Mutineer* (Quartet Books, 1978)

*Max Arthur, *Last Post* (Phoenix, 2005)

*Max Arthur ed., *Forgotten Voices* (Ebury Press, 2002)

Corelli Barnet, *The Great War* (BBC, 1979)

*Richard Holmes, *Tommy* (Harper Perennial, 2005)

Lyn Macdonald, *Somme* (Penguin, 1983)

*Ben McIntyre, *A Foreign Field* (Harper Collins, 2001)

*Richard Van Emden, *The Trench* (Bantam, 2002)

Diaries, letters and biography

*Alan Bishop and Mark Bostridge eds, *Letters from a Lost Generation* (Abacus, 1998)

Vera Brittain's War Diary, ed. Alan Bishop, *Chronicle of Youth* (Gollancz, 1981)

*Svetlana Palmer and Sarah Wallis, *A War in Words* (Pocket Books, 2003)

*Diary of an Unknown Soldier, *A Month at the Front* (Bodleian Library, University of Oxford, 2006)

*Michael Walsh, *Brothers in War* (Ebury Press, 2006)

Literary criticism and cultural commentary

*Adrian Barlow, *The Great War in British Literature* (Cambridge, 2000)

Bernard Bergonzi, *Heroes' Twilight* (Constable, 1965)

Paul Fussell, *The Great War and Modern Memory* (Oxford University Press, 1975)

*Dominic Hibberd, *Wilfred Owen* (Weidenfeld & Nicolson, 2002)

Collections

*Agnès Cardinal, Dorothy Goldman and Judith Hattaway, *Women's Writing on the First World War* (Oxford, 1999)

*Joyce Marlow ed., *The Virago Book of Women and the Great War* (Virago, 1999)

Drama

Alan Bleasdale, *The Monocled Mutineer* (Hutchinson, 1986)

Richard Curtis and Ben Elton, *Blackadder Goes Forth* (Penguin, 1989)

Joan Littlewood, *Oh! What a Lovely War* (Methuen, 1965)

Stephen MacDonald, *Not About Heroes* (Faber, 1982)

Miles Malleson, *Black 'ell* (1916)

Somerset Maugham, *For Services Rendered* (1982)

Frank McGuiness, *Observe the Sons of Ulster Marching Towards the Somme* (Faber, 1986)

Sean O'Casey, *The Silver Tassie* (1929)

George Bernard Shaw, *Heartbreak House* (1919)

George Bernard Shaw, *O'Flaherty V.C.* (1915)

Robert Cedric Sherriff, *Journey's End* (Heinemann, 1928)

Peter Whelan, *The Accrington Pals* (Methuen, 1982)

*Nick Whitby, *To the Green Fields Beyond* (Faber, 2000)

Poetry

*Rita Dove, *American Smooth* (*Not Welcome Here* Section) (Norton, 2004)

Brian Gardner ed., *Up the Line to Death* (Methuen, 1964)

Robert Giddings, *The War Poets* (Bloomsbury, 1988)

*Christopher Martin, *War Poems* (Collins Educational, 1990)

*The Alternative Book of First World War Poetry ed. V. Noakes, *Voices of Silence* (Sutton, 2006)

Catherine Reilly ed., *Scars Upon My Heart* (Virago, 1981)

Jon Silkin, *Men Who March Away* (ed. Parsons, 1965)

Jon Stallworthy ed., *The Oxford Book of War Poetry* (Oxford, 1984)

The Wordsworth Book of First World War Poetry (Wordsworth editions, 1995)

Brooke

Sassoon

Owen

Rosenburg

Gurney

Texts in translation

Henri Barbusse, *Under Fire* (Penguin, 1916)

*Agnès Cardinal, Dorothy Goldman and Judith Hattaway, *Women's Writing on the First World War* (Oxford, 1999)

*Marc Dugain, *The Officers' Ward* (Phoenix House, 1999)

Ernst Junger, *Storm of Steel* (Penguin, 1920)

*Svetlana Palmer and Sarah Wallis, *A War in Words* (Pocket Books, 2003)

Erich Maria Remarque, *All Quiet on the Western Front* (Vintage, 1929)

Your reading log

Keeping a record of your reading will be very important, especially as you will be dealing with a good many extracts. It is very important that you keep a detailed **Reading Log**; at the end of the course this will provide a very useful revision tool. Another useful thing to do would be to place all your reading in the shared context on a **timeline**.

Close reading for your AS English Literature course

Not only is it important that you read widely throughout the course, but you must also ensure that you develop the skills of **close reading**. You will need these skills in every answer you write and they underpin the whole of your AS English Literature course.

Close reading of a text will enable you to **analyse** and **explore** a writer's techniques – his or her choices of form, structure and language – and help you to:

■ respond fully to meaning or possible meanings of the text
■ gain understanding of the ways texts work
■ find textual evidence to support your interpretation.

If you are the kind of reader who does **not** read closely, you will only be able to offer a **skimpy** reading of your texts, based on **unsupported assertion**. This will not be sufficient for you to be successful in your AS English Literature course. Nor is there any point in counting numbers of syllables, making exaggerated claims for alliteration, or setting out a pattern of rhyme (ababcc, for example), unless this research is part of an analysis or exploration of the ways the writer's choices make meaning for you.

It is important that you adopt good reading habits:

■ You should read every whole text or extract three or four times in order to mine it thoroughly; the first reading will be for general impression, the subsequent ones will enable you to explore the writer's techniques fully.

■ Initially you will respond to subject matter and theme.

■ Then you need to move on to the ways the writer expresses the subject matter.

In order to analyse the ways writers write, these are some of the kinds of questions you should be asking yourself:

■ What kind of text is this?

■ When was this text written?

■ What is the subject matter?

■ Who is speaking and how does the writer use the idea of 'voice' in the text?

■ How does the writer use setting(s)?

■ How does the writer use ideas of time? (past, present, future)

■ How does the writer structure, organise and develop the ideas in the text?

■ Is there anything distinctive in the way the text is written? (structure, choices of vocabulary, sentence structures, variations in pace …)

■ Are there any patterns, repetitions of key ideas or images, uses of contrast?

■ What kinds of language are used? (formal, informal, descriptive, dialogue, and so on)

■ How has finding out more about the references and allusions in the text added to my understanding and interpretation?

■ Is the language all the same or does the writer use contrast?

■ What is the tone of the text?

■ What might be the writer's purpose in this text?

All the answers to these questions need to be related to your own interpretation of the text, and to your own making of meaning.

How your work will be assessed

Your wider reading in the poetry, prose and drama of World War One, as well as your knowledge and understanding of your chosen poetry text, will be assessed in Unit 1. You will write two essays in a two-hour examination. This unit carries 60% of AS or 30% of A2 marks. In Unit 2 (coursework) you will write two more essays, one on your prose text and one on your drama text. The folder as a whole will be about 2,500 words in length and carries 40% of AS or 20% of A2 marks.

All your work for the course will be assessed against four Assessment Objectives (AOs). These are:

AO1 Articulate creative, informed and relevant responses to literary texts, using appropriate terminology and concepts, and coherent, accurate written expression (*your ability to use your knowledge and understanding, to focus on the task, and to express yourself appropriately*).

AO2 Demonstrate critical understanding in analysing the ways in which structure, form and language shape meanings in literary texts (*your ability to explore the ways the writers' choices of form, structure and language influence the ways you interpret texts and make meaning*).

AO3 Explore connections and comparisons between different literary texts, informed by interpretations of other readers (*your ability to find links between the texts you read and to explore alternative readings*).

AO4 Demonstrate understanding of the significance and influence of the contexts in which literary texts are written and received (*your ability to assess where and how your texts fit into the shared context*).

These four Assessment Objectives are used to measure your achievement throughout the Specification and are organised by your examiners into a marking grid which is used to assess each piece of work that you do throughout your course. You, and your teachers, will be able to check your performance against the criteria in the grid. Each of the AOs is divided into 'bands' (see the table below).

If your work has the features of **Band 1** work – inaccurate, irrelevant, assertive – you will not be writing at the required standard for AS.

If your work is assessed as falling into **Band 2**, it is judged to be narrative and descriptive and rather generalised in its approach to text.

If your work is assessed as falling within **Band 3**, it means that you are starting to explore and analyse the texts and presenting your work in a coherent fashion.

If your work is assessed as falling into **Band 4,** it is coherent, cogent, mature and sophisticated and worthy of the highest grade.

Marking grid for Units 1 and 2

	Assessment Objectives			
	AO1	**AO2**	**AO3**	**AO4**
	AO1: Articulate creative, informed and relevant responses to literary texts, using appropriate terminology and concepts, and coherent, accurate written expression	**AO2: Demonstrate critical understanding in analysing the ways in which structure, form and language shape meanings in literary texts**	**AO3: Explore connections and comparisons between different literary texts, informed by interpretations of other readers**	**AO4: Demonstrate understanding of the significance and influence of the contexts in which literary texts are written and received**
Band 1	Candidates characteristically: ■ communicate limited knowledge and understanding of literary texts ■ make few uses of appropriate terminology or examples to support interpretations ■ attempt to communicate meaning by using inaccurate language.	Candidates characteristically: ■ identify few aspects of structure, form and language ■ assert some aspects with reference to how they shape meaning.	Candidates characteristically: ■ make few links between literary texts ■ reflect the views expressed in other interpretations of literary texts in a limited way.	Candidates characteristically: ■ communicate limited understanding of context through descriptions of culture, text type, literary genre or historical period.
Band 2	Candidates characteristically: ■ communicate some basic knowledge and understanding of literary texts ■ make simple use of appropriate terminology or examples to support interpretations ■ communicate meaning using straightforward language.	Candidates characteristically: ■ identify obvious aspects of structure, form and language ■ describe some aspects with reference to how they shape meaning.	Candidates characteristically: ■ make straightforward links and connections between literary texts ■ reflect the views expressed in other interpretations of literary texts in a basic way.	Candidates characteristically: ■ communicate some basic understanding of context through descriptions of culture, text type, literary genre or historical period.

	Candidates characteristically:	Candidates characteristically:	Candidates characteristically:	Candidates characteristically:
Band 3	■ communicate relevant knowledge and understanding of literary texts ■ present relevant responses, using appropriate terminology to support informed interpretations ■ structure and organise their writing ■ communicate content and meaning through expressive and accurate writing.	■ identify relevant aspects of structure, form and language in literary texts ■ explore how writers use specific aspects to shape meaning ■ use specific references to texts to support their responses.	■ explore links and connections between literary texts ■ communicate understanding of the views expressed in different interpretations or readings.	■ communicate understanding of the relationships between literary texts and their contexts ■ comment appropriately on the influence of culture, text type, literary genre or historical period on the ways in which literary texts were written and were – and are – received.
Band 4	■ communicate relevant knowledge and understanding of literary texts with confidence ■ present relevant, well-informed responses, fluently using appropriate terminology to support informed interpretations ■ structure and organise their writing in a cogent manner ■ communicate content and meaning through sophisticated and mature writing.	■ identify relevant aspects of structure, form and language in literary texts ■ confidently explore how writers use specific aspects to shape meaning ■ show a mastery of detail in their use of specific texts to support their responses.	■ explore links and connections between literary texts with confidence ■ communicate understanding of the views expressed in different interpretations or readings in a mature, sophisticated manner.	■ communicate a mature understanding of the relationships between literary texts and their contexts ■ comment in a sophisticated manner on the influence of culture, text type, literary genre or historical period on the ways in which literary texts were written and were – and are – received.

We now turn to an exploration of the detail of your studies. Each section in this book looks at a different part of your AS English Literature A course in more detail:

■ the set texts for Unit 1

■ coursework for Unit 2

■ wider reading in the three genres – poetry, prose and drama

■ how to prepare for the context question in your written examination

■ a sample examination paper and how to get the best possible marks in your answer.

We begin in the next chapter with a consideration of the set poetry text on the written paper.

We have considered:

■ the kinds of reading you will be doing

■ the choices you will be making

■ the skills you need to develop

■ how your work will be assessed.

2 How to approach the set text in Unit 1

Aims of the chapter:

- Introduces the poetry set text.
- Presents the relevant assessment objectives for this unit.
- Shows you the kinds of questions you will be asked in your examination.
- Discusses how you will be assessed in the examination.
- Considers the best and most effective ways to approach the study of your set text in this unit.

Choice of text

There are three poetry texts set for study on this paper; you will study **one** of them. We are going to look at what each one offers in terms of the poetry of World War One and at how each editor and selector approaches their task.

You will be studying one of the following texts.

Either

1 *Up the Line to Death: The War Poets 1914–1918* (published 1964)

This is an anthology selected and arranged by Brian Gardner. The editor has also written an **introduction** and provided **biographical notes** for each poet. He has chosen 141 poems which represent the work of 72 **male** poets. From the 1960s, Gardner looks back at the previous generation, and declares his intention to write a 'tribute' to the soldiers of World War One. He has arranged the poems in such a way as to tell the story of the war. In his introduction, he describes the book as a 'journey from Laurence Binyon's "The Fourth of August" to Philip Johnstone's "High Wood" ' and as 'a book written by men who either witnessed or took part in that journey'.

The book is organised into **sections** which reflect the 'journey', so that poems are grouped under the following headings:

Prelude	*Happy is England Now*	*Field Manoeuvres*
Tipperary Days	*To Unknown Lands*	*Home Front*
Death's Kingdom	*A Bitter Taste*	*Behind the Lines*
O Jesus Make it Stop	*At Last, at Last!*	*Epilogue*

Each section is introduced by a snippet of words from a popular World War One song.

In the introduction, Gardner goes on to cover topics such as the fellowship of the soldiers, the different kinds of poetry, the reputations of the poets, and the influence of the time of writing.

Or

2 *Scars Upon My Heart: Women's Poetry and Verse of The First World War* (published 1981)

In contrast to the all-male anthology edited by Brian Gardner, this anthology, edited by Catherine Reilly, consists of 125 poems written by 79 women. She states in her introduction that her research had established that of the 2,225 men and women who had had World War One poems published, 532 of them were women. However, the editor was concerned that these 532 women poets had never been represented in anthologies of World War One poetry. The publication of this anthology can be set in the context of the feminist movement and the rise of Women's Studies in universities in the 1970s and 1980s. The editor notes the 'received' view of the women's poetry as idealistic and ignorant of the realities of the war, but both she and the writer of the **preface**, Judith Kazantzis, claim that the common threads of this poetry are 'horror of war' and 'loss and mourning'. Certainly the poems invite the reader to share the experiences that blighted women's lives.

The poems are arranged alphabetically, by the poet's surname, with biographical notes at the end of the book.

Or

⚲ 3 *The Oxford Book of War Poetry* (published 1984)

Jon Stallworthy has chosen and edited this collection of poems. The collection as a whole includes war poems through time, from 900 BC to contemporary poets such as Seamus Heaney and Margaret Atwood. The section of the text that is set for study – from page 160 to page 225 – consists of about 60 poems about World War One. Only two of these poems are by women poets.

Stallworthy's introduction traces the development of war poetry and the wide range of feelings about and responses to conflict from *The Iliad*, to *Beowulf*, to Chaucer and the chivalric tradition, through the 18th and 19th centuries, the American Civil War, to World Wars One and Two. The poems are arranged chronologically by conflict, so that the collection can be regarded as a poetic history of warfare.

The editor provides some short notes and references.

To summarise:

All three texts offer you a rich selection of World War One poetry, but there are key differences between them in terms of the **kinds** of poetry chosen, the **time** of publication and the editor's **approach and purposes**:

▨ Gardner selects only **male** poets writing at the time of the war, and organises their poems **thematically** according to the chronology of the war. He sees his anthology as a 'tribute' to the soldier poets.

▨ Reilly selects only poems written by **women** and clearly states that her purpose is to give the female poets of World War One a platform and to disclose women's perspectives on the experience of the war and its aftermath.

▨ Stallworthy has compiled a collection of war poems that span the centuries. His aim is to show the ways attitudes to and feelings about war have changed through time. If you choose this option, you will study **only** the poems about World War One. The great majority of these poems are written by **male** poets.

⚲ 𝑖 🔍 Studying the poems in your chosen text

Once your poetry text is chosen, you must do all you can to make sure you are familiar with the whole anthology, and that you understand each poem.

You will need to study each poem individually, along with the collection as a whole. Here are some suggestions for how you could go about doing this:

1 For each poem:

▨ Look back to the section on close reading in Chapter 1 and use the prompts and questions to work with each poem.

▨ Make a note of your responses to the questions, the ways you interpret the poem and how it reflects experiences of World War One.

■ You should start a Reading Log where you record your responses to each poem. This may be organised in a paper file, or another way of doing this would be to use the online Reading Log provided for you. You can save this and add to it throughout your course. You can also print it out for revision.

2 For the whole collection:

■ Go on to consider how the individual poems connect and compare with each other, in terms of subject matter and style.

■ Look at the way the text is structured and explore why you think the editor chose to arrange it in this way.

■ Try arranging the poems in a different way and assess the changed impact that the new structure has on the reader.

The notes you assemble from these activities will help you to produce very useful notes for your revision.

■ The Assessment Objectives for Unit 1

When you have read and studied your poems closely, you need to consider the ways in which you will prepare for the examination. Clearly, your preparation needs to be informed by the way in which you will be assessed. We have looked at the Assessment Objectives (AOs) in some detail in Chapter 1, and you may wish to remind yourself of what they are and how they work.

For your set text, there are **three** relevant Assessment Objectives:

AO1 – *your ability to use your knowledge and understanding, to focus on the task, and to express yourself appropriately*

AO2 – *your ability to explore the ways the writers' choices of form, structure and language influence the ways you interpret texts and make meaning*

AO3 – *your ability to find links between the poems you study and to explore alternative readings.*

You will be assessed on your ability to meet all three assessment objectives, but you will need to remember that the **most important** Assessment Objective is **AO3** – your ability **to connect and compare the poems** as well as **to consider different interpretations.**

■ What kinds of questions will I have to answer in the examinations?

The three relevant Assessment Objectives are reflected in every question set on your chosen poetry text. You will be given a choice of two questions, and you will answer one of them. All the questions test the same Assessment Objectives.

Each question will set out a view which you are invited to consider. You will need to say how far you agree with the view in the question.

A few examples of the kinds of views that may be expressed in the questions are:

■ a named poem as the key to the collection
■ a named poem as an appropriate introduction to the collection
■ a named poem as an appropriate conclusion to the collection

- the collection has little variety
- the collection lacks coherence
- many of the poems in the collection have no literary merit.

You can make up your own questions using some or all of these suggestions, swap them with other students and attempt to answer each other's questions. This should help you to develop the receptive, open-minded approach to the ideas of others that is one of the keys to examination success.

Remember that you need to consider the view, saying how far you agree, through consideration and comparison of poems in the collection. Most questions invite you to consider two or three poems in some detail or to range more widely.

How will I be assessed in the examination?

Examiners will use the four-band marking grid to which you were introduced in Chapter 1. They will assess your essay using a mark scheme tailored to each question. This will relate to:

- the three relevant Assessment Objectives
- the four-band marking grid
- the key words of the question.

Summary

Advice for success

- Remember that this is still an English Literature examination. Although the questions on your set text will be testing Assessment Objective 3 in particular, meeting Assessment Objectives 1 and 2 is still vital to your success. You will need to be able to write clear, structured answers, have a secure knowledge of the text and show that you are able to analyse the writer's use of language and style.

- You will meet the Assessment Objectives if you produce a relevant answer which addresses the key words of the question you choose: the wording and construction of all the questions are designed to point you towards the appropriate Assessment Objectives.

- Look carefully at the Assessment Grids in Chapter 1: this is a detailed, generic version which applies to all questions. The examiners will be using the grids when they mark your set text answer: the descriptors for each level and Assessment Objective will give you some idea of what they will be looking for.

- You should try to develop the skills necessary for the construction of a balanced argument: these are vital because you will meet Assessment Objective 3 by writing a relevant answer to the question 'How far do you agree?'

- You should try to think for yourself when responding to your chosen set text question. Although it is not compulsory, you may refer to any critics you have read if you wish to. However, your own ideas are the most important: the question will invite you to express your answer in the first person.

- Remember that, as this is an open-book examination, there will usually be a question that requires you to focus on a specific poem or group of poems.

Link

If you turn to Chapter 8 you will see sample poetry questions on a specimen paper.

- It is important that you back up your ideas by close reference to the poetry when answering your set text question, but keep the quotations short: examiners know that a candidate who copies out large chunks of the text is probably struggling to cope.

- Remember that you are expected to be familiar with the whole of the poetry selection you have studied.

- Make the effort to read around the set text you are studying. Wider reading can provide important background information on your set poet in the context of World War One, and will give you the chance to consider other perspectives on the poetry which will help you to address Assessment Objective 3.

What to avoid

- Don't respond to the examination question by writing an account of a poet's life and times. A successful answer to the question might include some relevant biographical information, but it's important that you display your contextual knowledge through your knowledge of the poetry.

- Don't write an answer that wholly agrees (or disagrees) with the view that is set up for discussion in the question: such a one-sided, unbalanced response will be given a Band 2 mark, no matter how good your textual knowledge is, because you won't have met Assessment Objective 3.

- Don't abuse the open-book examination by copying anything out of the introduction or the notes included in your set text: the examiners will spot what you've done and they know that anyone who tries it must be desperate: unassimilated critical material is often a feature of Band 1 answers.

- Don't recycle your practice answers when you sit the examination. The questions are never the same as those set previously, so twisting an earlier essay in an attempt to fit it to a new question usually ends in disaster. You must approach each question afresh.

3 Approaching the coursework

Introduction

For Unit 2 you will be asked to present a folder of coursework that contains **two** pieces of writing: an essay on a **prose** text and another on a **drama** text. Both texts will come from the **shared context** of World War One literature. You will be given a list of ten prose texts and a list of three drama texts from which you make your choices. When you have studied your two chosen texts, you will then negotiate the two tasks with your teacher. Your teacher will make sure that both of your agreed tasks reflect the relevant Assessment Objectives.

A moderator, the representative of the Examination Board, will be assigned to approve the tasks that you have agreed with your teacher or to give advice when any changes need to be made to the tasks you have chosen. The total number of words that you will be asked to write for the two tasks together is between 2,000 and 2,500 words.

In this chapter we are going to:

- explore the opportunities offered by coursework for you to work in different ways

- look at each of the ten prose texts (from which you will have to choose the one you want to study and write about in your coursework)

- explore the kinds of tasks that are appropriate in order to reflect the relevant Assessment Objectives

- look at the three drama texts (from which you will have to choose the one you want to study and write about in your coursework)

- explore the kinds of coursework tasks that are appropriate in order to reflect the Assessment Objectives.

Coursework – a different way of working

Your coursework will give you opportunities to work in ways that are very different from the way you would prepare for an examination. You will need to make the most of these opportunities in order to gain the maximum marks for your coursework. You will plan and write your coursework by working through the following stages, each of which gives you the opportunity to make the most of your work.

1 Negotiating the task

Once your two coursework texts have been chosen, and you have read and studied them in detail, you will have time to think about **what particularly interests you** about the texts. Finding an appropriate **focus** for your writing is a crucial first step. Having taken it, you can then start to consider the kind of task you will negotiate with your teacher. Unlike the examination in Unit 1 where an examiner writes the questions, in the coursework you and your teacher are responsible for deciding the task. Of course, it must be constructed within the guidelines laid down by the Board; we will look at those guidelines towards the end of the chapter.

2 Research

Once you have agreed your task with your teacher and it has been approved by the moderator, you will have time and opportunity to carry out your own **research** on the topic you have chosen. You will need to organise yourself well and decide how you will keep the notes you take down in a systematic way so that they are of most use to you. You will, of course, need to keep a note of any sources that you consult, other than the primary text, as you will be expected to acknowledge these at the end of your essay.

3 Writing

When you are confident that you have done all the necessary reading and research, and have all the information that you require, you can turn to the actual writing of your essay. One advantage of writing coursework is that you can consult your teacher at any stage of the process. You will need to:

- plan carefully
- select the relevant material
- organise and structure your writing
- write the first draft.

You may wish to use the online planning tool to support planning your coursework.

You can, of course, show this draft to your teacher for comment, and you can then redraft your essay in the light of any advice or suggestions you are given.

4 Ensuring the quality of written communication and presentation

Your coursework gives you the opportunity to reconsider your ideas, and then draft and redraft your work. You will therefore be expected to present work that is well written, accurate and fluent, and well presented. If you choose to write your essays by hand, it is important that your writing is legible. If you choose to word-process your work (as most candidates do), it is important that you consider presentation and appearance. You should use a standard font that is clear and easy to read. You should use a font size no smaller than 12 points, and should not type your entire essay in italics or capitals.

🔍 The prose text

We are now going to look at each of the ten prose texts from which you will be choosing one to study and write about in your coursework. The texts cover the period 1918 to 2005; six are by female authors and four by male authors. You will choose **one** of these texts and write a coursework essay on it.

We will consider the texts (with the exception of the *Regeneration* **trilogy**) **chronologically**, in the order in which they were written.

1 The Return of the Soldier by *Rebecca West (1892–1983)*

This novel was written in 1918, during World War One.

Biography

Rebecca West was born Cicely Isabel Fairfield in London. She took her pen name from a character in a play entitled *Rosmersholm*, by the Norwegian playwright Henrik Ibsen, in which she had acted in her teens. This novel was her second book. She had a son with H.G. Wells in 1914, and married Henry Maxwell Andrews in 1930. She was made a Dame Commander of the Order of the British Empire in 1959.

Story

The Return of the Soldier is set in 1916. At the heart of the story is the loss of memory of the soldier referred to in the title, Chris Baldry. He has forgotten his wife and his marriage of ten years and remembers nothing after 1901. He remembers only the girl he was in love with in his youth, fifteen years ago. His beautiful house is described in great detail: his wife is always finely dressed. But the loss of memory from shell shock seems not simply a way of escaping from the war but also from the reality of his marriage. Margaret, his previous love, has a key role to play – she brings the news of his condition and, in the end, it is her sacrifice that 'cures' him so that he can return to both his wife and war.

Narrative viewpoint and structure

The story is told by one of the three women in the story, Jenny, the soldier's cousin. This is an interesting choice of narrator, and should this be your choice of text you would need to consider the effectiveness of the narrative viewpoint. Jenny lives with the soldier and his wife and knows both of them very well, especially Chris, with whom she has had a lifelong relationship. She is also clearly in love with him.

This is a short book of six chapters. There are interesting uses of contrast in characters, settings and lives. The story is told chronologically with the use of flashbacks.

Use of World War One context/gender/time

Rebecca West was clearly not a **combatant**, but she was someone who lived through the war and she was able to paint a picture of the effect of war on society and on those who wait at home. She also portrays the stress of a shell-shocked soldier sent home from the trenches. There is a sense of longing in the book to return to how life had been before the war. Margaret is the character who represents pre-war life, and the soldier had to give her up. West sees that the real tragedy of war was that it brought irrevocable changes throughout society.

The title focuses on a 'soldier', but the book concerns itself with three women and their experience.

This is an immediate and contemporary response to the ways World War One affected both combatants and those remaining at home.

2 Her Privates We *by Frederic Manning (1882–1935)*

This novel was written in 1929.

Biography

Frederic Manning was born in Sydney, Australia. A sickly child, he was educated at home. As a teenager, he became a close friend of Arthur Galton, Secretary to the Governor General who went home to England in 1898 and took Manning with him. Manning returned to Australia in 1900, but settled in England in 1903 and, still a sickly man, turned to writing for a living. He lived in a vicarage in the countryside, and did not volunteer in 1914 because he thought that he would fail the medical. But in 1915 he enlisted in the Shropshire Light Infantry and became Private 19022. He was selected for officer training but dismissed for drunkenness. He went to France in 1916 as a private, and an 'elderly' one at that – he was 34. He joined the secondary stages of the Somme battle. His war as a private lasted four months; he returned at Christmas 1916 for officer training. The four months as a private on the Somme are the background for this novel.

Later in the war he resigned his commission; there were more problems with drink. After the war, he went back to writing. He was still in poor health. A publisher, Peter Davies, urged him to write his memoirs – hence this book. He clearly preferred to set down his experiences in fiction.

The book was originally called *The Middle Parts of Fortune* and was published privately and anonymously by 'Private 19022'. Its realism and strong language meant that it was suppressed, and an expurgated version was published in 1930 under the title *Her Privates We*. The original text was not published until 1977.

Story

Most of the action takes place behind the reserve lines in the Somme valley in northern France during the late summer of 1916. The central character is a man called Bourne, who stands out from the others because he is different. He is a thoughtful and quiet man, older and educated. He is friendly with the NCOs and drinks with the sergeants. He can speak French, and is used as an interpreter. Clearly the character is based on Manning himself.

The book is a detailed account of life in a self-contained world with its own laws and values. The focus is narrow, but the book is generally acclaimed as having universal appeal. Manning describes the men as preoccupied with food, drink, sex and idleness as they wait for battle. They tolerate the officers, but have no enthusiasm for battle and no noticeable patriotism, no faith in the leaders or even interest in the war. This was certainly no stereotypical view of war.

Narrative viewpoint and structure

Manning writes in the third person. The perspective is impartial and detached.

The book has 18 chapters, each introduced by a quotation from Shakespeare. (Each of the titles used is a quotation from Shakespeare's *Hamlet*.) It is written as a chronological narrative.

Use of World War One context/gender/time

This novel, written ten years after the war, was based on the writer's personal experience as a male **combatant** in World War One. The events happened; the characters are fiction.

3 Not So Quiet *by Helen Zenna Smith (1896/1901–1985)*

This novel was written in 1930.

Biography

Helen Zenna Smith was a pseudonym for the popular British journalist and author Evadne Price. She was born off the coast of Australia to British parents. Her birth date is the subject of some dispute – the National Union Catalogue gives it as 1896, but her husband of 54 years said that it was 1901. (Certainly the narrator of *Not So Quiet* would have been born around 1896/7.) Price was educated in New South Wales and England.

Albert Marriott, a publisher, asked her to write a spoof of *All Quiet on the Western Front*. It was to be called *All Quaint*, and to be written from a woman's point of view. She managed to persuade him to publish an account of a woman's experience of war instead. She had no personal experience of the Front, so she persuaded Winifred Young, who had kept diaries of her time as an ambulance driver in France, to let her write a novel faithful to Young's experiences. She locked herself up with the diaries for six weeks and wrote this book to critical acclaim – including the Prix Severine in France, because, as the awarders of this prize said, it was 'the novel most calculated to promote international peace'. There were four sequels: *Women of the Aftermath* in 1931, *Shadow Women* in 1932, *Luxury Ladies* in 1933, and *They Lived with Me* in 1934.

Story

The novel is about the experiences of six English women with an average age of 21 as they drive field ambulances of wounded men picked up by trains at the Front. Hospitals were set up just behind the fighting zones, and volunteer drivers (like the volunteer aid detachment, VAD) tended to be the daughters of the patriotic upper-class families who could afford to subsidise their voluntary activities. There is no doubt that they suffered severe hardship doing the dirty work of society. They would drive for weeks at a time on three hours' sleep, eating very little. They all became experts at driving the screaming wounded at night with the lights off. The cabs were open so they were often freezing cold. Key ingredients of the story are: the main character's move from volunteer ambulance driving; a breakdown; home leave; deliberate rejection of class privilege; and her return to the Front as a cook's assistant with working-class WAACs (Women's Army Auxiliary Corps). In her introduction to the novel, Jane Marcus calls it a 'brutal, tense and angry narrative'.

Narrative viewpoint and structure

There are **multiple** voices here. First there is the imitation of *All Quiet on the Western Front*, and then the turning of another woman's diaries into fiction. There are also the voices of 'Mother' and Mrs. Evans-Mawnington, which are conjured up through the consciousness of the main character.

The novel is written in 12 chapters. Letters are used in fragments and written up as mini-dramas through extensive use of dialogue. The present tense provides the framework, and it is written chronologically.

Use of World War One context/gender/time

Twelve years after the war, Helen Zenna Smith makes use of personal war experience (even if not her own, it represents the real experience of women) to extend the range of and to challenge preconceptions about the form and content of female writing about the war. She describes the aftermath of battle wounds, mutilations and piles of dead bodies, replacing stereotypical 'feminine' squeamishness with realistic depictions of the ways that strong and assertive women faced the horrors resulting from trench warfare.

4 Memoirs of an Infantry Officer *by Siegfried Sassoon (1886–1967)*

This novel was written in 1930.

Biography

Siegfried Sassoon was born into a wealthy family in Kent. He studied at Marlborough College and then at Clare College, Cambridge. He left there without graduating in 1907 and proceeded to live the life of a country gentleman, spending time hunting, playing cricket and golf and writing poetry. He had some poems printed privately, but they had little impact on the literary scene.

Aged 28 at the onset of war, he enlisted as a cavalry trooper, first in the Sussex Yeomanry, and then transferred to the Royal Welch Fusiliers (where he met and became a friend of Robert Graves) as an officer in May 1915. He was given the nickname 'Mad Jack' for his fearless courage on the Western Front, where he often volunteered to run night raids. He was awarded the Military Cross in June 1916 for getting a wounded man back to the British lines while under fire. Wounded himself in April 1917, he was sent to England for recuperation. He was also increasingly angry about the conduct of the war, and the result of this was that he published a letter in *The Times* stating his view that the war was being deliberately prolonged by the authorities.

Only the intervention of Robert Graves, who convinced the Review Board that Sassoon was suffering from shell shock, prevented his punishment by court martial. He was sent to Craiglockhart Hospital in Edinburgh to recover, and it was there that he met Wilfred Owen. After Craiglockhart he was sent to Palestine, then on to France, where he was again wounded and sent home.

After the war he wrote three volumes of a classic fictional autobiography, loosely based on his immediate pre-war and war experiences: *Memoirs of a Fox-Hunting Man* in 1928, followed by *Memoirs of an Infantry Officer*, and, finally, *Sherston's Progress* in 1936. (He later published three volumes of his real autobiography.)

Story

Memoirs of a Fox-Hunting Man covers George Sherston's early life, his joining up, and his home leave in 1916. *Memoirs of an Infantry Officer* then takes up the story, covering many of the experiences which Sassoon describes in his war poems. Obviously the genre, the mode of presentation, is different from the poems, and the tone of the writing avoids their bitterness. The book concentrates on the battle scenes. The fighting before the Hindenburg Line in April 1917 when Sassoon (Sherston) is wounded is described. The book ends with his arrival at Craiglockhart Hospital, after his protest.

Narrative viewpoint and structure

The novel is written in the first person, with a character called George Sherston as the speaker. We assume that Sherston's experiences are Siegfried's (and, indeed Sassoon confirms this in his later book, *Siegfried's Journey*). However, the personal and family circumstances of Sherston and Sassoon are different, and Sherston is not a poet but a country gentleman of leisure who, before, his transformation into an infantry officer, devotes his time to hunting and cricket.

Sassoon does not adopt the objective, detached approach of Robert Graves in his book *Goodbye to All That* and we are constantly aware of his own involvement in the scenes he portrays.

The novel is written in ten chapters and most of them have subdivisions. George Sherston's story is told chronologically.

Use of World War One context/gender/time

Written 12 years after the end of the war, this book is written from and reflects on the personal experience of a male combatant at the Front in 1916/17. It describes the atmosphere of the time and the conditions of life in the trenches.

5 Strange Meeting *by Susan Hill (1942–)*

This novel was published in 1971.

Biography

Susan Hill was born in Scarborough and educated first at Scarborough Convent School and then at grammar school in Coventry. She read English at King's College London. Her first novel was published in 1961. She is a prolific writer of prose, plays and non-fiction. She is married to the Shakespeare scholar, Stanley Wells, and lives in Oxfordshire.

Looking at her novels one can trace an interest in relatively well-to-do families that are dysfunctional, broken or about to be broken. Throughout her work there are also disturbing images of death, loss and haunting.

This novel comes relatively early in her writing career. In an interview she talks of how her own family history, as well as hearing Benjamin Britten's *War Requiem*, gave her the impetus to write. The title of the novel is taken from a poem by Wilfred Owen that Britten set in his *War Requiem*, about the ghosts of a British and a German soldier meeting. However, it took eight years of research into the war before she felt ready to write. Then she went to stay at Aldeburgh, the seaside town in Suffolk where the composer Benjamin Britten lived until his death in 1976, in order to write the novel. She said that she found the miles of uninterrupted beach as well as the wild weather provided her with an appropriate context for writing. At the time it was an ambitious and unusual choice of topic for a woman writer.

Story

John Hilliard is on sick leave and finds his time at home with his family difficult. He then returns to find his battalion tragically changed after action and massive casualties. Then David Barton arrives – he is a young man from a loving, supportive and communicative family who possesses great charm. Hilliard and Barton's encounter is a 'strange meeting'; they are opposites, but they develop a strong and deep friendship. There are intense and affecting battle scenes. David Barton is killed and John Hilliard severely wounded. At the end of the novel, Hilliard visits the Barton family and discovers some hope for the future.

Narrative viewpoint and structure

The novel has an **omniscient narrator**. It also makes extensive use of letters, as well as a good deal of dialogue.

The novel is **structured** in three parts. Part One is about Hilliard's time at home and his meeting with Barton once back in France away from the lines. Part Two sees them arriving at the Front, and Part Three starts as the soldiers await the battle which sees Barton killed.

Use of World War One context/gender/time

This novel is written by a female **non-combatant** over 50 years after the end of the war. Her own interest in the subject, as well as her family's involvement, led her to write the novel. She conducted intensive research before writing an **imaginative reconstruction** of soldiers at the Front during the war.

6 Regeneration *by Pat Barker (1943–)*

This novel, the first of a trilogy, was published in 1991.

Biography

Pat Barker was born in Thornaby-on-Tees. She was educated at the London School of Economics, where she read International History, and

Fig. 1 *'Paths of Glory' by C.R.W. Nevinson*

at Durham University. She taught history and politics until 1982. She began to write in her mid twenties, encouraged by Angela Carter. Her early novels focused on the harsh lives of working-class women in the north. The *Regeneration* trilogy was partly inspired by her grandfather's experience of the trenches. *Regeneration* has been made into a film; *The Eye in the Door* won the Guardian Fiction Prize; and *The Ghost Road* won the Booker Prize for Fiction. Pat Barker was awarded the CBE in 2000.

Reading a Pat Barker novel is never a comfortable experience. She explores controversial, often taboo subjects. The trilogy has been called brutal (even brutish) and horrific; Barker believes that we can only understand physical and mental distress when we are up close to it. The reader is not spared the detail of men in acute distress or of scenes in the trenches. When she received the Booker Prize in 1995, Pat Barker said: 'The Somme is like the Holocaust. It revealed things about mankind that we cannot come to terms with and cannot forget. It can never become the past'.

Nor does Barker ignore the complexities of her characters. For example, Sassoon wants the war to end and is savagely critical of the politicians, but he is also a brave soldier and a great leader. Rivers is a kind and sensible doctor, but it is he who sends the men back to the war and to death. And one of the most complex characters is the fictional Billy Prior, who moves across all boundaries of class and sexuality.

Story

This is a war story where there are no battles except those for men's minds.

The central characters are Siegfried Sassoon and Dr Rivers. They are both real people and Pat Barker used a good deal of her research into Rivers' papers in the book.

Sassoon and Rivers meet at Craiglockhart Hospital where Sassoon is sent after making his public declaration, attacking the continuation of the war. Rivers was a social anthropologist before the war, studying nerve regeneration. He is a thoughtful and intelligent man who has to deal not only with his patients but also with his own conscience, as he tries to make men sane enough to go back to the Front. Rivers has to unlock the things his patients are trying to forget, reliving their worst memories with them. Sassoon's early recovery comes about because he tries to remember what others try to forget. He also sees that he has reached safety and left his men in danger.

The character Billy Prior is a patient of Rivers'. After time at the Front, he suffers from mutism and asthma. He is a working-class man who has achieved officer status. His relationship with Sarah Lumb introduces the reader to some interesting aspects of life on the Home Front for women – jobs, home life and relationships. Rivers tries hypnosis on Billy.

Sassoon meets Wilfred Owen at the hospital and becomes a mentor to him on his poetry. A deep relationship develops. When Sassoon decides to return to the Front, Owen is strongly affected.

The novel ends with Rivers reflecting on Sassoon. The reader reflects on how and why the soldiers are 'regenerated'.

Narrative viewpoint and structure

The novel has an omniscient narrator. It is structured in four main parts and 23 chapters. Events are told chronologically, with flashbacks coming from the treatment of the patients as well as Rivers' previous life. Key themes are madness, homosexuality, masculinity and parenthood.

Use of World War One context/gender/time

This novel (like the other two books in the trilogy) was written by a female non-combatant over 70 years after the end of the war. It is based on extensive research, especially into the work of Rivers – and on imaginative reconstruction. Barker uses real people as well as her own fictional inventions.

7 The Eye in the Door *by Pat Barker*

This novel, the next part of the trilogy, was written in 1993.

Story

This book follows on from *Regeneration*, continuing the stories of Rivers, Prior, Sassoon and Owen, ending some time before the conclusion of the war later in the year. It explores the climate of radical pacifism in London in 1918, covering a broad social range of characters. Wilfred Owen is not from a public school. Then there is Billy Prior, who moves across class and sexual boundaries with confidence and who comes more into prominence in this novel. At this time, there was a real possibility of defeat for Britain, and the two scapegoat groups for the government and the public were pacifists and homosexuals. The novel reflects the double lives lived by many. The 'eye' is the symbol of the paranoia threatening to destroy society.

Narrative viewpoint and structure

Again we have the omniscient narrator. This book is driven by action and a good deal of dialogue. Description is kept to a minimum and a good deal of tension comes from the doctor/patient interviews. The book goes some way to answering the questions left unanswered by *Regeneration* – for example: What happens to Sassoon? How does Rivers resolve the conflicting and contradictory issues of war and medicine? What resolution is there for Billy Prior and Sarah? There are answers, but there are also fresh questions posed.

Fiction has a greater part to play here than the blend of fact and fiction in the previous book. This gives Barker more freedom to explore Billy Prior, her fictional creation, as well as to set up interesting contrasts between Billy's intense and random bisexuality, Rivers' detachment from sexual issues and Sassoon's homosexuality. She also concentrates on some of the contradictions of the war.

A key question to ask yourself is: as the middle book of the trilogy, how far does this book stand alone?

The book is written in three parts and 21 chapters.

8 The Ghost Road *by Pat Barker*

This novel was written in 1995.

Story

Sassoon has only a minor role to play in this story; the main players are Rivers and his patients Billy Prior and Wilfred Owen, who return to the Front as his 'test cases', cured of their shell shock. In August 1918, Prior travels through London and says his farewell to Rivers. In France, millions of men are engaged in brutal trench warfare and all are 'ghosts in the making'. Again Barker is exploring the possible relationships between fictional and real characters. Rivers, for example, has real concern for Prior's safety and realises that he acts as a father figure to his patients.

Billy Prior is now engaged to Sarah and has found some sort of resolution in his life. He still takes all kinds of risks, however, and not least sexual ones. He breaks his own rule that he never pays for sex; perhaps this is a symbol of his capitulation to the inevitability of death in battle – a fate he shares with Wilfred Owen at the end of the book.

Narrative viewpoint and structure

The novel is written in three parts and 18 chapters.

There is interesting use of different and contrasting settings – London and the Front for example; and also, as Rivers suffers from a high temperature and fever, he remembers his time in a community of former headhunters, and starts to reconsider the time he spent there and to make connections with his current life.

In this novel, Barker explores interactions and relationships between social classes, between doctors and patients, men and women, and men and men.

Of particular note is the way in which Barker constructs the ending of this book. A set-piece battle scene is set against the death of Hallett, where Rivers realises that the chorus of 'shotvarfet' means that the war is 'not worth it'. The battle scene is presented as it happened rather than through fragments of memory of various patients, and gives an account of the attempted crossing of the Sambre-Oise on 4 November 1918. The death of Wilfred Owen is witnessed by the shot and dying Billy Prior.

9 Birdsong *by Sebastian Faulks (1953–)*

This novel was published in 1993.

Biography

Faulks was educated at Wellington College and then Emmanuel College, Cambridge University. He has worked on the *Independent* and the *Guardian* and is a Fellow of The Royal Society of Literature. *Birdsong* is the middle book in a loose trilogy spanning World Wars One and Two; the other two books are *The Girl at the Lion d'Or* and *Charlotte Gray*. In his writing, Faulks has made the human costs of love and war his special subject. He was awarded the CBE in 2002.

Story

The majority of the book concentrates on Stephen's life before and during the war; it also focuses on Elizabeth, his granddaughter, and her attempts to find out about his experiences. Stephen is a lonely, brooding yet charismatic character.

Making excellent use of researched detail, Faulks writes a vivid account of the trenches. The accumulation of detail combined with the tone of emotional restraint creates a story of great pathos. Faulks depicts the sheer horror above ground and the clammy claustrophobia of the tunnels below with clinical precision. Worthy of note is the set-piece description of the opening of the battle of the Somme.

The novel ends with the Armistice and the birth of a new generation.

Narrative viewpoint and structure

The book has an omniscient **third-person narrator**, but is set in three different time frames – pre-war, during World War One and the late 1970s – with a soldier and his granddaughter taking the main roles in each.

The book consists of seven sections which cover three different time periods. They are:

- France 1910
- France 1916
- England 1978
- France 1917
- England 1978/9
- France 1918
- England 1979.

In the pre-war section, Stephen has a passionate affair with the wife of his host in France. In 1916 he is a lieutenant in the army on the Somme. His outfit is responsible for planting mines under the German trenches and towards the end of the novel he becomes trapped underground (echoes of Owen's *Strange Meeting*?) with Jack Firebrace, a former miner.

The structure of the novel frames Stephen's wartime life with that of a civilian (his granddaughter) towards the end of the 20th century, contrasting her self-interest with Stephen's wider sacrifice.

Use of World War One context/gender/time

This is a novel written by a male writer, 75 years after the end of the war. It is based on extensive research of the subject and takes the form of an imaginative reconstruction.

10 A Long Long Way *by Sebastian Barry (1955–)*

This novel was published in 2005.

Biography

Sebastian Barry was born in Dublin in 1955. His play *The Steward of Christendom* was first produced in 1995 and won many awards. The play concerns a Dublin policeman serving the Crown – the policeman is the father of Willie Dunne (the main character of this novel).

Barry not only took the story of his own grandfather's experiences in World War One, but he also conducted extensive research in order to write his novel. *A Long Long Way* was shortlisted for the Man Booker Prize for Fiction.

Story

The novel deals with an issue that has been virtually airbrushed from Irish history – the involvement of Ireland in the British army during World War One. The book tells the story of Willie Dunne, the son of a Dublin policeman, and his service in the Royal Dublin Fusiliers until his death in 1918. It is both a brutal and a poetic book, which spares no detail in its depiction of the squalor of life at the Front for both privates and officers. It shows Ireland at a crossroads; the Royal Dublin Fusiliers suffer horrors abroad while their native city is in turmoil. They are fighting in an army that is often guilty of racism against the Irish, while back at home they are regarded as traitors.

The book explores the Easter Rising in Ireland, a significant political moment, and its effect on the Irish men fighting in foreign lands for the King of England – the doubts and divisions caused by the situation.

Narrative viewpoint and structure

The novel has an omniscient narrator; the story is also told through several letters and a postcard. The focus of the writing is on the camaraderie and humour of Willie and his regiment, as well as on the cruelty and sadness of war and the divided loyalties that many Irish soldiers felt.

The book is divided into three parts, with 23 chapters with subdivisions.

Use of World War One context/gender/time

A Long Long Way was written 87 years after the end of the war by a male Irish writer. It is an imaginative reconstruction based on extensive research and family stories.

Writing about your chosen novel

Having reviewed all the possible choices, we are going to turn to the writing of the essay.

1   Studying the text

You will need to read your chosen novel several times so that you know and understand the text and can analyse and explore the ways the writer's choices of structure and language shape your response.

You will need to consider, discuss and make notes on the following aspects of the text:

■ the writer's purposes

■ the structure of the novel

■ the narrative viewpoint

■ interesting aspects of language and imagery

■ key themes

■ characters.

2   Finding a focus for your essay

When you know your novel well, then, with your teacher's help, you will need to find an aspect of the text that interests you and about which you can construct an appropriate task. An appropriate task might focus on any of the aspects that you were invited to consider in the list above.

Your teacher will help you to construct a task that enables you to:

■ write an informed and relevant response to your text using coherent and accurate written expression (AO1)

■ show that you can analyse the ways the writer's choices of structure and language shape meaning (AO2)

■ explore your interpretation of the text (AO3)

■ show your understanding of how the text reflects the World War One context (AO4).

3   Interpretation or transformation?

Here you have another choice to make. For this essay you can:

■ **either** write a conventional essay that explores some aspect of the text, like characterisation, theme or structure, with a focus on your **personal informed interpretation** of the text

■ **or** you can do a piece of **creative transformational** writing, such as an alternative ending, a 'missing' chapter, a letter from or diary of a character in the novel. This piece will be assessed against the same Assessment Objectives as a more conventional essay, so it will need to reflect the writer's style, the way characters are realised, and so on.

The following are some suggestions as to how you might approach each of these options.

Activity

Write as many tasks as you can on the aspect of your chosen text which interests you. You can do this individually, with a partner or in a group. You can then share your tasks with your partner or the group, and get your teacher to check that they are appropriate.

The personal informed interpretation

- If your choice of novel were *Strange Meeting* by Susan Hill, an appropriate task might be:
  'Explore the ways in which Susan Hill portrays the families of Barton and Hilliard.'
- Or, if you had chosen *Not So Quiet* by Helen Zenna Smith, it might be:
  'Explore the ways Smith portrays women in *Not So Quiet*.'
- Or, if you had chosen *Birdsong* by Sebastian Faulks, it might be:
  'Examine the structure of *Birdsong* and assess the impact of the structure on the ways you interpret and respond to the book.'
- Or, if you had chosen *The Return of the Soldier* by Rebecca West, it might be:
  'Explore the effects of West's choice of narrator on the ways you interpret the novel.'

Activity

Think of as many ways as you can of writing a creative, transformational task on your chosen novel. You can do this individually, with a partner or in a group. You can then share your ideas and discuss them with your teacher.

The creative, transformational piece

This is your opportunity to move out from the actual text and create your own piece of writing. But remember that your writing needs to have developed from the text and to read as though it could be an integral part of it.

Examples of possible tasks:

- If you had chosen to study *Strange Meeting*, you could write The Epilogue.
- If you were studying *The Return of the Soldier*, you could compose Margaret's Diary.

The drama text

Now we will turn to the second piece of writing in the coursework folder. We begin by looking at the choices of the drama text.

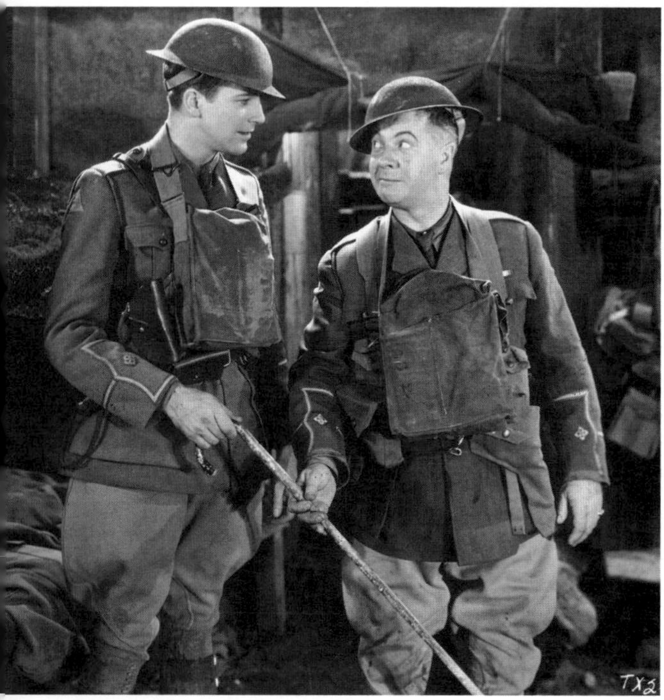

Fig. 2 *A performance of **Journey's End***

There is a choice of three drama texts set for study in this coursework unit; you will be studying one of them. The following are the choices, in order of the time of composition.

1 Journey's End *by R.C. Sherriff (1896–1975)*

R.C. Sherriff was educated at Kingston Grammar School in Kingston upon Thames, and in 1914 was working as an insurance clerk. He resumed his work as an insurance adjuster from 1918 to 1928 at the Sun Insurance Company, London, on his return from the war.

During the war, he served as a captain with the 9th East Surrey Regiment. He was wounded at Passchendaele near Ypres and spent six months in hospital. This play, which was first performed in December 1928 with Laurence Olivier playing the part of Stanhope, is based on his war experiences.

Journey's End is set in 1918 on the Western Front, where the Germans were once more preparing a massive offensive against the British army in France.

It is a play in three acts with a single setting – a dugout. The action is condensed into a short length of time, from Monday to Thursday (18 to 21 March 1918). There is a small cast of male characters, including the flawed hero, Stanhope. Sherriff provides very detailed stage directions. The play has much to say about heroism, cowardice, comradeship, horror and class.

Summary

This is a play written by a male combatant ten years after the end of the war, drawing on his own experiences. Its focus is on trench life for soldiers under attack.

2 The Accrington Pals *by Peter Whelan*

Peter Whelan was born and grew up in Stoke-on-Trent. He has written seven plays for the Royal Shakespeare Company. *The Accrington Pals* was first performed in 1981 by the Royal Shakespeare Company at The Warehouse in London.

At the heart of the play is the Pals Battalion, raised in the early months of the war in response to Kitchener's call for a voluntary army. Friends from all walks of life in Accrington and neighbouring towns enlisted together to form a battalion with a local identity. The battalion suffered devastating losses in their first major action – the attack on the Serre on 1 July 1916, the opening day of the Battle of the Somme.

The inspiration for the play, according to Whelan, came first from his own family. Having found a snapshot of his mother taken while she was a volunteer female lumberjack during World War One, Whelan comments: 'I suppose what I couldn't believe was that my mother as I knew her then – stout, middle-aged and living entirely for her family – had ever experienced such release. Doors had once been opened and then slammed shut, as they had been for millions of young women in that war. And through the doors they had glimpsed tantalising freedoms as well as unimaginable horrors.' Whelan also read Martin Middlebrook's book, *The First Day on the Somme*, and his interest was caught by a short paragraph about Accrington which described how the townsfolk surrounded the Mayor's house, trying to find out what had happened – suspicious of and challenging authority.

The action of the play takes place between 1914 and 1916 and is based on real events. The characters are fictional. There is dramatic contrast between the volunteers going off to war with confidence and optimism and the women left behind. Whelan presents a close-knit group of women dealing with the changes to their lives that the war has brought.

Fig. 3 *From a production of **The Accrington Pals***

The play is written in two acts. There are scenes in camp in England and in France, in the Accrington recruiting office and in Sarah's backyard, but the majority of the action is either at May's stall or in her kitchen.

Summary

The play was first performed 63 years after the end of the war. It was written by a male playwright who had researched and imaginatively reconstructed what happened to the Accrington Pals and their families. The strength of the women in the community is an especially important ingredient of the play.

3 Not About Heroes *by Stephen MacDonald*

This play was first performed at the Edinburgh Festival in 1982 and won a Fringe First Award. A revised edition of the play was published in 1986. The text is based on the poetry and letters of Owen and Sassoon. Its purpose is to tell the truth about the war and its horrors. It is an anti-war play with no scenes of violence.

Fig. 4 *From a production of* **Not About Heroes**

Not About Heroes is a play in two acts about the friendship of Sassoon and Owen. These are the only two characters in the play. The story of 1917 and 1918 is narrated by Sassoon from his country house as he relives significant incidents from that time. The play's structure is therefore based on flashbacks. The setting, framed by Sassoon's home, moves from Edinburgh to Craiglockhart, to Scarborough, to London, to Flanders.

The play traces the initial meeting of the men in Craiglockhart Hospital, where Owen has been sent with nervous shock and to where Sassoon has been sent after he published his Declaration. At first the play shows us that Owen is in awe of his hero and that Sassoon is rather distant, but they soon form a strong bond, and the play goes on to portray their intense relationship. At the heart of the relationship is the common bond of poetry and the creative process. In one key scene, we see Owen's growing confidence as a poet and the two men in the process of composing *Anthem for Doomed Youth*.

Summary

This play, written by a male playwright, was first performed 64 years after the end of the war. Based on the key sources of poetry and letters, it is an intimate poetic and literary play which imaginatively reconstructs the Owen/Sassoon friendship.

Writing about your chosen drama text

Having reviewed the three possible choices of drama texts, we will now turn to a consideration of the kind of task you need to construct.

1   Studying the text

    You will need to read your chosen drama text several times so that you know and understand the text and can explore and analyse the ways the writer's choices of structure and language shape your responses.

You will need to consider, discuss and make notes on the following aspects of the text:

- the writer's purposes
- the structure and the setting of the play
- interesting aspects of language
- key themes
- characters.

2 Finding a focus for your essay

When you know your chosen play well, then, with your teacher's help, you will need to find an aspect of the text that interests you and about which you can construct an appropriate task. An appropriate task might focus on any of the aspects that you were invited to consider in the list above.

Your teacher will help you to construct a task that enables you to:

- write an informed and relevant response to your text using coherent and accurate written expression (AO1)
- show that you can analyse the ways the writer's choices of structure and language shape meaning (AO2)
- explore your interpretation of the text and make connections with other texts (AO3)
- show your understanding of how the text reflects the World War One context (AO4).

3 Comparison with the prose text or connection to other World War One plays

Here you have another choice to make. For this essay, you can:

- **either** place the chosen play in its dramatic context, reaching out to your wider reading in World War One plays
- **or** connect the chosen play to the chosen prose text.

Whichever task you choose, you will focus on aspects of the drama text such as theme, structure or characterisation.

- If the two chosen texts were *Regeneration* and *Journey's End*, then your task might be:

  'Explore the ways Sherriff uses setting for dramatic effect in *Journey's End*.' Then:

  Either
  - Compare the ways *Journey's End* and other World War One plays you have read use settings.

  Or
  - Compare the ways Sherriff uses setting with the ways Barker uses the enclosed environment of Craiglockhart Hospital in *Regeneration*.

- Or, if the two chosen texts were *Return of the Soldier* and *The Accrington Pals*, then your task might be:

  'Explore the ways Whelan presents women in his play.' Then:

  Either
  - Compare the ways *The Accrington Pals* and other World War One plays present women.

Activity

Write as many tasks as you can on the aspect of your chosen text that interests you. You can do this individually, with a partner or in a group. You can then share your tasks with your partner or the group, and get your teacher to check that they are appropriate.

Or

– Compare the ways Whelan presents the women left at home with the ways West presents the female characters in *Return of the Soldier.*

Summary

Success in your coursework will depend on:

■ careful choice of texts

■ the negotiation of two clearly focused tasks

■ planning your time so as to make the best use of the opportunities offered by coursework

■ developing a clear line of argument

■ maintaining a focus on the writers' choices of form, structure and language

■ developing the points you make and supporting them with close reference to the text and appropriate quotation

■ your personal engagement with and independent thinking about your texts.

4   Tackling wider reading in poetry

Aims of the chapter:

- Studies and explores the connections between a selection of World War One poems, written across time and circumstance and by both men and women within the shared context.

- Discovers how the experience of World War One changed the ways poets write.

- Draws meaning from the poems, recognising key features of content and style as well as range and variety.

- Discovers how the Assessment Objectives may be applied to the poetry.

Introduction

This chapter and the two chapters that follow introduce you to ways of reading widely in the literature of World War One, and prepare you for the context question of Unit 1.

This chapter focuses on how to approach your wider reading in **poetry**; the two chapters that follow deal with **prose** and **drama**.

Poetry, as you will have realised, is the dominant genre in World War One writing. As well as those poems that are commonly anthologised, thousands of poems were written by ordinary people, including soldiers, keen to record their experiences in a form that suited itself to people on the move, or living in cramped circumstances. A recent anthology, *Voices of Silence, The Alternative Book of First World War Poetry* edited by Vivien Noakes, has attempted to gather together much of this 'lost' poetry. Scouring hospital gazettes, private scrapbooks and primitive trench newspapers, the editor has retrieved a wealth of poetry written by the less well-known or gifted poets, whose work has largely been forgotten. She acknowledges that much of the poetry she includes 'could more accurately be described as verse', but quite justifiably claims that the book 'evolved into the story of the experience of the Great War told in verse by those who were there'.

We have already looked at the **set poetry texts** in Chapter 2, but you should remember that the **two set texts** that you do **not** choose can provide the basis for your wider reading. The poems chosen for close study in this chapter do **not** appear in any of the three set text collections.

Victorian and Edwardian poetry about war and conflict

It is always dangerous to generalise, and in your reading you will always be able to find evidence to question generally accepted opinions, but it is true to say that the experience of the Great War changed not only **attitudes to war**, but also **ways of writing** about it, challenging previous conventions and traditions.

It is worth spending some time looking at the ideas and themes of pre-1914 poetry on the subject of war and conflict, and we will start by looking at the famous Victorian poem, 'The Charge of the Light Brigade' by Alfred, Lord Tennyson. This poem expresses Victorian ideas and values in a most idealistic way. In Victorian times, it was accepted that the poem **celebrated** a military **disaster**. The soldiers do not question that they should do their duty, showing extreme courage in the face of an impossible situation and performing the ultimate sacrifice for their country. It is possible to read the poem as echoing with celebration and triumph through the commands – *Charge!*; the strong active verbs – *rode, volleyed, thundered*; and the rhythm of galloping horses. As a 21st-century reader, you may find that it is perhaps capable of ambiguity and of other interpretations.

Link

The context question is dealt with in Chapter 7.

The Charge of the Light Brigade

I

Half a league, half a league,
  Half a league onward,
All in the valley of Death
  Rode the six hundred.
'Forward, the Light brigade!
Charge for the guns!' he said:
Into the valley of Death
  Rode the six hundred.

II

'Forward, the Light Brigade!'
Was there a man dismayed?
Not though the soldier knew
  Someone had blundered:
Theirs not to make reply,
Theirs not to reason why,
Theirs but to do and die:
Into the valley of Death
  Rode the six hundred.

III

Cannon to the right of them,
Cannon to the left of them,
Cannon in front of them
  Volleyed and thundered;
Stormed at with shot and shell,
Boldly they rode and well,
Into the jaws of Death,
Into the mouth of Hell
  Rode the six hundred.

IV

Flashed all their sabres bare,
Flashed as they turned in air
Sabring the gunners there,
Charging an army, while
  All the world wondered:
Plunged in the battery-smoke
Right through the line they broke;
Cossack and Russian
Reeled from the sabre-stroke
  Shattered and sundered.
Then they rode back, but not
  Not the six hundred.

V

Cannon to the right of them,
Cannon to the left of them,
Cannon behind them
  Volleyed and thundered;
Stormed at with shot and shell
While horse and hero fell,
They that had fought so well
Came through the jaws of Death,
Back from the mouth of Hell,
All that was left of them,
  Left of six hundred.

VI

When can their glory fade?
O the wild charge they made!
  All the world wondered.
Honour the charge they made!
Honour the Light Brigade,
  Noble six hundred!

Alfred, Lord Tennyson

Fig. 1 *'The Charge of the Light Brigade' by Caton Woodville. How similar are this painting and Tennyson's poem in their interpretation of the event?*

And here is a poem from the time of the South African (Boer) war 1899–1902. The Boer War began as a struggle between the British and the Dutch 'Boer' settlers for control of diamond and gold deposits in the Orange Free State and Transvaal. After early defeats the British army, reinforced by troops from other parts of the Empire, claimed victory in 1900. The Boers, however, continued the conflict using guerrilla tactics, and it was only when the British adopted a scorched earth policy, burning farms and rounding up women and children into concentration camps, that they finally crushed the Boers. This poem not only promotes similar values to those of the Tennyson poem, but also makes an attempt to represent the reality of battle.

Vitai Lampada

There's a breathless hush in the Close tonight –
    Ten to make and the match to win –
A bumping pitch and a blinding light,
    An hour to play and the last man in.
And it's not for the sake of a ribboned coat,
    Or the selfish hope of a season's fame,
But his Captain's hand on his shoulder smote –
'Play up! play up! and play the game!'

The sand of the desert is sodden red, –
    Red with the wreck of a square that broke; –
The Gatling's jammed and the Colonel dead,
    And the regiment blind with dust and smoke.
The river of death has brimmed his banks,
    And England's far, and Honour a name,
But the voice of a schoolboy rallies the ranks:
    'Play up! play up! and play the game!'

This is the word that year by year,
    While in her place the School is set,
Every one of her sons must hear,
    And none that hears it dare forget.
This they all with a joyful mind
    Bear through life like a torch in flame,
And falling fling to the host behind –
    'Play up! play up! and play the game!'

Sir Henry Newbolt

Fig. 2 *An army surgeon tends the wounded in the field at Colenso in 1899, during the Boer War*

Let's take a little time to consider our response to these poems.

- How do we, as 21st-century readers, respond to the ways that Tennyson plays down the 'blunder'? And do we not find more than slightly ridiculous the idea of a 'schoolboy' rescuing a situation by seeing a bloodthirsty battle as a game of cricket?

Our response, however, is **not** the response of the late 19th- or early 20th-century reader, for whom the ideals and ideas of **service**, **sacrifice**, **loyalty** and **heroism** were uppermost.

- **Compare** the poems and make notes about the ways in which they present visions of service, sacrifice, loyalty and great heroism.
- Can you trace their influence in any of the World War One poems you have read?

Perhaps the key thing to remember about these poems and the poetry of the time is that it was taught to the young men who went off to war in 1914. This is the literary **context** they carried with them into the trenches.

This is also the kind of poetry **challenged** and forever **changed** by the experience of the Great War.

World War One poetry

We are now going to look in detail at some poetry from and about World War One. Using a chronological approach, you will consider:

- poetry at the start of the war
- trench poetry from mid war
- retrospective female poetry in the years after the war
- poetry written at the time of World War Two which looks back to World War One
- and finally, poetry written in the 21st century about World War One.

You need to keep a record of your discoveries so that you develop a reading diary – this may be in a file on paper or you could do this using the online Reading Log in the **e-resource.**

1 Poetry at the start of World War One

At the start of the war, there was a good deal of evident enthusiasm – 750,000 men volunteered in the first eight weeks. Protecting and fighting for their land seemed uppermost in the minds and hearts of English men – quite literally. When Edward Thomas was asked why he was prepared to fight, he picked up a clod of soil, held it out and said, 'Literally, for this'. In an essay published in 1914, Rupert Brooke described the feelings of an 'Unusual Young Man' (clearly himself) when he heard the news that war had been declared:

His astonishment grew as the full flood of 'England' swept him on from thought to thought. He felt the triumphant helplessness of a lover. Grey, uneven little fields, and small ancient hedges rushed before him, wild flowers, elms and beeches, gentleness, sedate houses of red brick, proudly unassuming, a countryside of rambling hills and friendly copses. He seemed to be raised high, looking down on a landscape compounded of the western view from the Cotswolds, and the Weald, and the high land in Wiltshire, and the Midlands seen from the hills above Prince's Risborough. And all this to the accompaniment of tunes heard long ago, an intolerable number of them being hymns.

This is an interesting description of thoughts and feelings as war is declared. Brooke treats the news as a time of 'revelation' in his life. Look at how he describes his standpoint as 'raised high'. Is this a reference to his 'English Heaven'? And another echo of his poem 'The Soldier' (number V in the sonnet series) comes in his choice of *England* rather than *Britain*, as well as in the representation of countryside surroundings. He shows himself moved in a religious way, and he celebrates those feelings.

Brooke's *1914 and Other Poems* was published by Sidgwick & Jackson Ltd in 1915. It opens with the famous sonnet sequence '1914', one of which (number IV, 'The Dead') we are going to look at in detail. Brooke worked at the five sonnets on and off during the early months of his time in the Anson Battalion (Royal Naval Division). He did consider them to be unfinished, saying, 'God, they're in the rough, these five camp-children – four and five are good enough, and there are phrases in the rest'. 'The Soldier' was quoted by Dean Inge when preaching in St Paul's on Easter Sunday 1915 and evoked great popular interest. The news of Brooke's death came a week later and he became hero, victim and martyr. His sonnets represent what England felt or wanted to feel in 1914 and have achieved mythic status.

Fig. 3 *Rupert Brooke*

Extract A

IV The Dead

These hearts were woven of human joys and cares,
  Washed marvellously with sorrow, swift to mirth.
The years had given them kindness. Dawn was theirs,
  And sunset, and the colours of the earth.
These had seen movement, and heard music; known
  Slumber and waking; loved; gone proudly friended;
Felt the quick stir of wonder; sat alone;
  Touched flowers and furs and cheeks. All this is ended.

There are waters blown by changing winds to laughter
And lit by the rich skies, all day. And after,
  Frost, with a gesture, stays the waves that dance
And wandering loveliness. He leaves a white
  Unbroken glory, a gathered radiance,
A width, a shining peace, under the night.

_____

Rupert Brooke

Questions

AO1: Developing an informed response to the text

▪ What thoughts and feelings is Brooke expressing in this poem?

AO2: Understanding how structure, form and language shape meaning

▪ Explore the language which Brooke uses to express his thoughts and feelings.

▪ Assess the appropriateness of the sonnet form.

▪ Examine the ways he uses the structure.

AO3: Exploring connections, comparisons and the interpretations of other readers

▪ Compare this sonnet with the others in the *1914* sequence.

■ **Further reading**

In your wider reading from the early part of World War One, you might include work by the following writers:

- ■ Herbert Asquith
- ■ Laurence Binyon
- ■ John Freeman
- ■ W.W. Gibson
- ■ Julian Grenfell
- ■ W.N. Hodgson
- ■ Charlotte Mew
- ■ Alice Meynell
- ■ Jessie Pope
- ■ Charles Sorley
- ■ August Stramm
- ■ Georg Trakl
- ■ Robert Ernest Vernede
- ■ Mary Webb.

■ Compare the sonnet with other poems written at the start of the war; you may wish to start with Julian Grenfell's 'Into Battle'.

■ Trace connections in ideas, themes, subject matter.

■ What have you discovered about similarities and differences between this poem and other early war poems?

■ Compare this early Brooke poem with the 'Fragment', written just before Brooke's death; make a note of the differences you have found.

■ Charles Hamilton Sorley said of Brooke's *1914*, 'That last sonnet sequence … which has been so praised, I find … over-praised. He is far too obsessed with his own sacrifice, regarding the going to war of himself (and others) as a highly intense, remarkable and sacrificial exploit, whereas it is merely the conduct demanded of him (and others) by the turn of circumstances … . He has clothed his attitude in fine words: but he has taken the sentimental attitude.'
How do you respond to this interpretation of Brooke's sonnet sequence?

AO4: Understanding the significance and influence of contexts

■ How does this poem reflect the context of the early years of the war? Consider both subject matter and style.

Make sure you keep your notes on this poem and its connections in your Reading Log.

2 Trench poetry

In this section we are going to look at poetry written by soldier poets during the war, and we shall focus on Sassoon and Owen in particular. Clearly, you will want to read widely in the poetry written during the war: Rosenberg, Graves, Blunden, Sorley, Thomas, to name but a few – and don't forget the international perspective.

Soldiers writing their poems at war changed the country's view of battle, leaving a legacy of horror. And, as we have said previously, they changed the language of poetry.

The list quoted below, provided by Paul Fussell in his book *The Great War and Modern Memory*, illustrates the change in poetic vocabulary that occurred because of poets' real experiences with war.

Everyone knew what Glory was, and what Honor meant …

We can set out this 'raised', essentially feudal language in a table of equivalents:

A friend is a	comrade	The draft-notice is	the summons
Friendship is	comradeship or fellowship	To enlist is to	join the colors
A horse is a	steed or charger	Cowardice results in	dishonour
The enemy is	the foe or the host	Not to complain is to be	manly
Danger is	peril	To move quickly is to be	swift
To conquer is to	vanquish	Nothing is	naught
To attack is to	assail	Nothing but is	naught, save
To be earnestly brave is to be	gallant	To win is to	conquer
To be cheerfully brave is to be	plucky	One's chest is one's	breast
To be stolidly brave is to be	staunch	Sleep is	slumber
Bravery considered after the fact is	valor	The objective of an attack is	the goal

The dead on the battlefield are	the fallen	A soldier is a	warrior
To be nobly enthusiastic is to be	ardent	One's death is one's	fate
To be unpretentiously enthusiastic is to be	keen	The sky is	the heavens
The front is	the field	Things that glow or shine are	radiant
Obedient soldiers are	the brave	The army as a whole is	the legion
Warfare is	strife	What is contemptible is	base
Actions are	deeds	The legs and arms of young men are	limbs
To die is to	perish	Dead bodies constitute	ashes or dust
To show cowardice is to	swerve	The blood of young men is	the red/sweet wine of youth

Certainly in many of the trench poems there is a clear sense of 'lived experience'. The poet David Jones referred to life for the soldier becoming more 'relentless … mechanical … sinister … impersonal', and, like other poets, his aim was to tell the truth to upset 'bloodthirsty civilians and those who falsely glorified the war'.

The two poems that follow – 'The Chances' by Wilfred Owen and 'A Working Party' by Siegfried Sassoon – tell of their experiences in a plain, direct style.

Extracts B

The Chances

I mind as 'ow the night afore that show
Us five got talkin', – we was in the know.
'Over the top tomorrer; boys, we're for it.
First wave we are, first ruddy wave; that's tore it!'
'Ah well,' says Jimmy, – an' 'e's seen some scrappin' –
'There ain't no more nor five things 'as can 'appen:
Ye get knocked out; else wounded – bad or cushy;
Scuppered; or nowt except yer feelin' mushy.'
One of us got the knock-out, blown to chops.
T'other was 'urt, like, losin' both 'is props.
An' one, to use the word of 'ypocrites,
'Ad the misfortoon to be took by Fritz.
Now me, I wasn't scratched, praise God Almighty,
(Though next time please I'll thank 'im for a blighty)
But poor young Jim, 'e's livin' an' 'e's not;
'E reckoned 'e'd five chances, an' 'e 'ad;
'E's wounded, killed, and pris'ner, all the lot,
The bloody lot all rolled in one. Jim's mad.

Wilfred Owen
First published 1919

Did you know?

Here is an explanation of some of the slang and military terms used by both poets:

- *Blighty* – soldiers' slang for home or England and also the name given to a wound that ensured a return to Blighty, hence the phrase 'lucky blighter'
- *Cushy* – soldiers' slang for easy or comfortable
- *Dug-out* – a roofed shelter dug into the walls of a trench
- *Fritz* – like *boche* and *hun*, soldiers' slang for Germans
- *Knocked out* – like pushing up daisies, pegging out; soldiers' slang for dying
- *Mushy* – soldiers' slang for emotionally overwrought
- *Props* – legs.

Fig. 4 *'The Harvest of Battle' by C.R.W. Nevinson*

A Working Party

Three hours ago he blundered up the trench,
Sliding and poising, groping with his boots;
Sometimes he tripped and lurched against the walls
With hands that pawed the sodden bags of chalk.
He couldn't see the man who walked in front;
Only he heard the drum and rattle of feet
Stepping along barred trench-board, often splashing
Wretchedly where the sludge was ankle-deep.

Voices would grunt 'Keep to your right – make way!'
When squeezing past some men from the front line:
White faces peered, puffing a point of red;
Candles and braziers glinted through the chinks
And curtain-flaps of dug-outs; then the gloom
Swallowed his sense of sight; he stopped and swore
Because a sagging wire had caught his neck.

A flare went up; the shining whiteness spread
And flickered upward, showing nimble rats
And mounds of glimmering sandbags, bleached with rain;
Then the slow silver moment died in dark.
The wind came posting by with chilly gusts
And buffeting at corners, piping thin
And dreary through the crannies; rifle-shots
Would split and crack and sing along the night,
And shells came calmly through the drizzling air
To burst with hollow bang below the hill.

Three hours ago he stumbled up the trench;
Now he will never walk that road again:
He must be carried back, a jolting lump
Beyond all need of tenderness and care.
He was a young man with a meagre wife
And two small children in a Midland town;
He showed their photographs to all his mates,
And they considered him a decent chap
Who did his work and hadn't much to say,
And always laughed at other people's jokes
Because he hadn't any of his own.

That night when he was busy at his job
Of piling bags along the parapet,
He thought how slow time went stamping his feet
And blowing on his fingers, pinched with cold.
He thought of getting back by half-past twelve,
And tot of rum to send him warm to sleep
In draughty dug-out frowsty with the fumes
Of coke, and full of snoring weary men.

He pushed another bag along the top,
Craning his body outward; then a flare
Gave one white glimpse of No Man's Land and wire;
And as he dropped his head the instant split
His startled life with lead, and all went out.

30 March 1916 Siegfried Sassoon
Written while in the Front Line during my first tour of trenches

Questions

AO1: Developing an informed response to the text

▪ Describe what is happening in each poem.

▪ What are the thoughts and feelings presented in each poem?

AO2: Understanding how structure, form and language shape meaning

▪ What do you notice about the language each poet has chosen to describe the events and present thoughts and feelings?

▪ How does each poet use form and structure to shape meaning? Explore Owen's use of direct speech and compare it with Sassoon's way of telling a story.

AO3: Exploring connections, comparisons and the interpretations of other readers

▪ Explore the similarities and differences of these two poems, considering both subject matter and style.

▪ What links can you find to other trench poems you have read?

▪ Compare these poems with some of the World War One poems by women.

▪ How do you respond to the view that these two poems are too brutal and realistic and lack subtlety to be effective war poems?

▪ In 1936, W.B.Yeats omitted Owen from the *Oxford Book of Modern Verse*, claiming he considered him 'unworthy of the poets' corner of a country newspaper'. He said, 'he is all blood, dirt and sucked sugar stick'. How do you respond to his comments?

AO4: Understanding the significance and influence of contexts

▪ How typical do you find these two examples of trench poetry?

▪ How do these poems reflect the time of writing and the gender of the writers?

3 The women poets

We turn now to look at women's writing during and about World War One. Before the war there was already evidence of unrest and of a general movement that sought more freedom – in terms of education, work and participation in politics – and social independence for women. The suffragettes were part of this movement.

Further reading

Read the other trench poets and female poets writing later in the war, such as:

▪ Richard Aldington
▪ Edmund Blunden
▪ Vera Brittain
▪ May Wedderburn Cannan
▪ Albert Ehrenstein
▪ Robert Graves
▪ Ivor Gurney
▪ Winifred Letts
▪ Rose McCaulay
▪ Herbert Read
▪ Isaac Rosenberg
▪ Alan Seeger
▪ Edward Thomas
▪ Guiseppi Ungaretti.

Fig. 5 *'For King and Country' by Edward F. Skinner*

Many women forged new ways of living during the war as they took on traditional male work – see D.H. Lawrence's short story *Tickets Please* (women working on public transport) or Pat Barker's *Regeneration* trilogy (women doing factory/munitions work). Women like Vera Brittain volunteered for nursing and often travelled to France.

As we established in Chapter 2, when writing about *Scars Upon My Heart*, women's World War One poetry was largely neglected until later in the 20th century. It is a poetry characterised by loss, grief and patience, but it would be wrong to accept this as the stereotype of women's poetry. Women's lives were often revolutionised by the war as they took on new roles and responsibilities and found new freedoms, and these experiences are also reflected in the poetry. Sometimes – with poets like Jessie Pope – it is hectoring and based on propaganda. Where women write about experience at the Front, of course, it is obviously imagined rather than based on real experience.

Here is a poem written by May Cannan after the war.

Extract C

Fig. 6 *May Cannan*

Perfect Epilogue
Armistice Day 1933

It's when the leaves are fallen I think of you,
And the long boulevards where the ghosts walk now,
And Paris is dark again save for one great star
That's caught and held in the dark arms of a bough

And wonder, among them are two a girl and boy
Silent, because their love was greater than song,
Who whisper 'farewell' and whisper 'if it's for ever';
And did not know, poor ghosts, for ever could be so long.

It's when the leaves are fallen I think of you,
And if you're lonely too, who went with the great host;
And know that Time's no mender of hearts but only
Still the divider of Light and Darkness, Ghost.

May Cannan

■ Questions

AO1: Developing an informed response to the text
- What event or series of events is the poem describing?
- What are the thoughts and feelings being expressed?

AO2: Understanding how structure, form and language shape meaning
- How does Cannan structure her poem so as to express the thoughts and feelings?
- What use does she make of past and present?
- What effect do the images of light and dark have?
- Explore the language she uses and its effects.

Questions

AO1: Developing an informed response to the text
- What event or series of events is the poem describing?
- What are the thoughts and feelings being expressed?

AO2: Understanding how structure, form and language shape meaning
- How does Cannan structure her poem so as to express the thoughts and feelings?
- What use does she make of past and present?
- What effect do the images of light and dark have?
- Explore the language she uses and its effects.

AO3: Exploring connections, comparisons and the interpretations of other readers
- What connections can you make between this poem and other poems by female writers that you have read?
- What differences and what similarities have you noticed in terms of subject matter and style?
- How do you respond to the view that, as non-combatants, women cannot write effective war poetry?
- Read some other poems written retrospectively and compare them with Cannan's poem.

AO4: Understanding the significance and influence of contexts
- How does this poem reflect the post-war context?
- How does it present the female perspective?

Further reading

Read other women poets and poets writing after the war, such as:
- Vera Brittain
- Margaret Postgate Cole
- Elizabeth Daryush
- Eleanor Farjeon
- Helen Hamilton
- Marie Carmichael Stopes
- Sara Teasdale
- Iris Tree
- Katharine Tynan.

4 Looking back from World War Two

As World War Two approached, poets such as Herbert Read reflected on the current situation with apprehension, looking back to the experience of the Great War.

Herbert Read was a literary and art critic. He fought in France during World War One. He wrote this poem in 1944.

Extract D

To a Conscript of 1940

A soldier passed me in the freshly fallen snow
His footsteps muffled, his face unearthly grey;
And my heart gave a sudden leap
As I gazed on a ghost of five-and-twenty years ago.

I shouted Halt! And my voice had the old accustomed ring
And he obeyed it as it was obeyed
In the shrouded days when I too was one
Of an army of young men marching

Into the unknown. He turned towards me and I said:
'I am one of those who went before you
Five-and-twenty years ago: one of the many who never returned,
Of the many who returned and yet were dead.

We went where you are going, into the rain and the mud;
We fought as you will fight
With death and darkness and despair;
We gave what you will give – our brains and our blood.

We think we gave in vain. The world was not renewed.
There was hope in the homestead and anger in the streets
But the old world was restored and we returned
To the dreary field and workshop, and the immemorial feud

Of rich and poor. Our victory was our defeat.
Power was retained where power had been misused
And youth was left to sweep away
The ashes that the fires had strewn beneath our feet.
But one thing we learned; there is no glory in the deed
Until the soldier wears a badge of tarnished braid;
There are heroes who have heard the rally and have seen
The glitter of a garland round their head.

Theirs is the hollow victory. They are deceived.
But you, my brother and my ghost, if you can go
Knowing that there is no reward, no certain use
In all your sacrifice, then honour is reprieved.

To fight without hope is to fight with grace,
The self reconstructed, the false heart repaired.'
Then I turned with a smile, and he answered my salute
As he stood against the fretted hedge, which was like white lace.

Herbert Read

Further reading
- Peter Porter, 'Somme and Flanders'
- Vernon Scannell, 'The Great War'.

Questions

AO1: Developing an informed response to the text
- Explore what is happening in the poem.
- What thoughts and feelings does the speaker express?

AO2: Understanding how structure, form and language shape meaning
- How does the poet's choice of language help to present his thoughts and feelings?
- Explore the ways he uses form and structure.
- Look at the ways Read uses his own war experience (and its aftermath) to structure his poem.

AO3: Exploring connections, comparisons and the interpretations of other readers
- Compare this poem with other retrospective poems written later in the century, such as Scannell's 'The Great War' or Porter's 'Somme and Flanders'.
- Compare this poem with poems written during World War One.
- What differences and similarities do you notice?
- How do you respond to the view that Read's poem is too much like a lecture to be effective poetry?

AO4: Understanding the significance and influence of contexts
- Explore how this poem uses the context of another war to reflect on experiences of World War One.

5 Late 20th- and 21st-century poetry

World War One continues to provide the subject matter for poetry in the late 20th and early 21st centuries; you may wish to consider why this is.

An interesting sequence of poems is to be found in *American Smooth*, written by the American poet Rita Dove and published in 2004. The sequence consists of eight poems and is called *Not Welcome Here*. It features the true story of a group of African Americans, also members of a jazz band, desperate to enlist to fight in World War One. At the time the American armed forces were segregated and there was reluctance to send these soldiers to Europe. The French, however, sent for them, and the 369th was the first regiment to arrive. Its achievements were legendary – the longest time in continuous combat (191 days) and many, many medals (170 individual Croix de Guerre). It was the first regiment to fight its way to the Rhine in 1918.

Extract E

Here is one poem from the sequence.

Alfonzo Prepares to Go Over the Top (Belleau Wood, 1917)

A soldier waits until he's called – then
moves ass and balls up, over
tearing twigs and crushed faces,
swinging his bayonet like a pitchfork
and thinking anything's better
than a trench, ratshit
and the tender hairs of chickweed.
A soldier is smoke
waiting for wind; he's a long corridor
clanging to the back of a house
where a child sings
in its ruined nursery…

    and Beauty is the
gleam of my eye on this gunstock and my spit
drying on the blade of this knife
before it warms itself in the gut of a Kraut.
Mother, forgive me. Hear the leaves? I am
already memory.

Rita Dove

Link

Britain's long-lasting interest in World War One is also considered in Chapter 5.

Fig. 7 *Croix de Guerre*

Further reading

Read some of these:

- The rest of the sequence *Not Welcome Here*
- Ted Hughes, 'Six Young Men'
- Philip Larkin, 'MCMXIV'
- Michael Longley, 'Wounds'
- Owen Sheers, 'Mametz Wood'.

Questions

AO1: Developing an informed response to the text

- What is happening in this poem?
- What are the thoughts and feelings expressed in the poem?

AO2: Understanding how structure, form and language shape meaning

- How do Dove's choices of language and structure enable her to express those thoughts and feelings?

AO3: Exploring connections, comparisons and the interpretations of other readers

- Compare this poem with the other poems about World War One soldiers in the sequence *Not Welcome Here*.
- Compare the poems with the trench poems written during the war itself. What similarities and what differences do you notice?
- How do you respond to the claim that Dove 'reaches straight to the heart of experience so that emotion rings true'?

AO4: Understanding the significance and influence of contexts

- How does this poem reflect its 21st-century context?

Summary

- In this chapter we have looked at poetry from and about World War One from the inception of the war to the present day. The experience of World War One changed both the content and the conventions of poetry. Through the 20th and into the 21st century poets have continued to 'write the war' and reshape it according to their own context.

5   Tackling wider reading in prose

Aims of the chapter:

- Studies a range of extracts from novels and memoirs about World War One, considering the variety of form used by writers.

- Finds meaning in the extracts, identifying key features of content and style.

- Finds connections between the extracts and wider reading and considers the ways the writers use context.

- Traces intertextuality, considering notions of truth, authenticity and realism.

- Explains how the Assessment Objectives can be applied to your reading.

Link

For more information on the context question and non-fiction writing, see Chapter 7.

Link

See Chapter 3 for a detailed overview of the ten prose texts.

Introduction

Literature and life

In his important and influential book, *The Great War and Modern Memory*, Paul Fussell notes that 'life feeds materials to literature while literature returns the favour by conferring forms on life'. How writers shape the raw material of World War One experience into literature will concern us throughout the chapter. We will examine how prose writers make choices of genre, form and techniques to convey experiences of and thoughts and feelings about World War One; and we will trace influences and connections (**intertextuality**) through time and across cultures and gender.

Fiction and non-fiction

In this chapter we concentrate on fiction, but we will pay attention to some **memoirs**. Chapter 7, the **context question** chapter, explores all kinds of non-fiction writing – cultural commentary, diaries, letters, biography, and so on – while this chapter focuses on fictional writing.

Overlap with coursework texts

In your coursework essays for Unit 2, you will choose to study one prose text from the Board's suggested ten. Obviously any or all of the other nine texts provide material for wider reading. Throughout this chapter, the ten texts are indicated by *; they are not given a great deal of attention here because they have been described in some detail in Chapter 3.

Structure of the chapter

We are going to look at prose writing in the following categories:

- 20th-century male writers
- memoirs
- 20th-century female writers
- writing from other countries
- 21st-century writers.

First we look briefly at fiction and its major themes before the outbreak of war.

Fiction before World War One

The writers

Prose fiction before the war was dominated by writers such as Arnold Bennett and John Galsworthy, whose *Forsyte Saga*, a study of a middle-class family's life, was half finished in 1914. The insecurities of the middle classes also formed the subject matter of E.M. Forster's *Howard's End*, which was published in 1910. In this book, two families clash but are eventually reconciled. It is the house after which the novel is named that represents stability and the continuity of English life. The novelist's key concerns seem to be: relationships, cultural life, landscape and the importance of place. The novels of D.H. Lawrence, who came into prominence just before the war, shared these preoccupations and developed other related themes – to the importance of the English landscape he added the threat of industrialisation, and to the study of relationships he added the emancipation of women and the urge for self-development.

One example of the merger of these themes in prose ficion is the short story *Tickets Please*, which Lawrence wrote in 1919. We see this picture of the girls who took over the jobs of the ticket collectors on the Nottingham trams during the war:

> This, the most dangerous tram-service in England, as the authorities themselves declare, with pride, is entirely conducted by girls, and driven by rash young men, a little crippled, or by delicate young men, who creep forward in terror. The girls are fearless young hussies, in their ugly blue uniform, skirts up to their knees, shapeless old peaked caps on their heads, they have all the sang-froid of an old non-commissioned officer. With a tram packed with howling colliers, roaring hymns downstairs and a sort of antiphony of obscenities upstairs, the lasses are perfectly at their ease.

Key themes

So at the start of the war, the major preoccupations of fiction writers were:

■ England
■ landscape and the land
■ mechanisation
■ the role of women.

It will be interesting to see how these themes were sustained, adapted, changed or abandoned by writers after 1914, as they absorbed the impact of World War One into their writing.

■ 20th-century male writers

Attitudes to war

The first novel to reflect public reaction to the war was published in 1916 – this was *Mr. Britling Sees It Through* by H.G. Wells. Wells was a pacifist, but thought that the Allied cause was just. His novel shows the effect of the war on a liberal and professional family living in some comfort in Essex. Soon after the war, *Tell England* by Ernest Raymond (1921) was published. This was an account of the Gallipoli expedition by an Anglican priest who had been there. This book was more celebratory of what it considered to be a 'just war', concerned to praise the patriotic commitment of those who fought and died. It also emphasises the link between the public schools, with their stress on Christianity and military training, and the idea of the cheerful sacrifice of youth.

Such patriotic fervour can be compared with the anti-war sentiments of D.H. Lawrence, as expressed in his novel *Kangaroo* (1923). In the chapter called 'The Nightmare' he wrote an autobiographical account of wartime England. He claimed:

> From 1916 to 1919 a wave of criminal lust rose and possessed England, there was a reign of terror, under a set of indecent bullies like Bottomley of John Bull and other bottom-dog Members of the House of Commons.

As you read widely in the prose written about World War One, make a record of the writers' attitudes to and thoughts and feelings about the war.

Fiction or memoir?

As you read widely you will notice the overlap between fiction and memoir. Many of the writers in the years after the war tried first of all to set down their experiences in the form of fiction. The interplay, overlap or tension between fiction and memoir is a thread that runs through this chapter. You will need to think about terms such as **realistic**, **true** and **reliable**, and about how you and other readers use them. As a student of literature, your concern is to explore the **ways** writers **shape** their **materials**. Clearly in this particular area of literature, history and real events form part of that material. Sometimes writers are shaping their **own experiences**, at other times they are relying on research, and **imaginative reconstruction**. Your job as a student of **literature** is to examine choices of genre, form and language and to explore the ways they convey thoughts, feelings and ideas to you, the reader; it is **not** to make judgements about the status of a text as **historical evidence** as a historian would.

We will look specifically at memoirs in the next section, but it is important to note that many of the men who went on to write memoirs of their war experiences tried to shape such material into fiction first. Sassoon, for instance, wrote *Memoirs of a Fox-Hunting Man* (1928), a novel with George Sherston as its main character, before writing his memoirs.

Richard Aldington wrote *Death of a Hero* (1929), a novel telling the life story of George Winterbourne, a young painter who grew up in the Victorian era. Winterbourne enjoyed the freedoms of pre-war London, then joined the army and was killed a few days before the Armistice. Years later (1941) Aldington wrote his memoirs, *Life for Life's Sake*. Robert Graves tried to write a novel about his war experiences, but finally decided to record them in the form of a memoir, *Good-bye to All That*.

Other fiction

Other key male writers of fiction in the 20th century are:

Sebastian Faulks, *Birdsong*★ (1993)

Ford Madox Ford, *Parade's End* (1924–8)

Frederic Manning, *Her Privates We*★ (1930)

Henry Williamson, *How Dear is Life* (1954)

Read the following two extracts carefully. They both focus on recruitment. The first is from *Mr. Britling Sees It Through* and the second comes from *Tell England.* Then answer the questions that follow.

Extract A (i)

The great 'Business as Usual' phase was already passing away, and London was in the full tide of recruiting enthusiasm. That tide was breaking against the most miserable arrangements for enlistment it is possible to imagine. Overtaxed and not very competent officers, whose one idea of being very efficient was to refuse civilian help and be very, very slow and circumspect and very dignified and over-bearing, sat in dirty little rooms and snarled at this unheard-of England that pressed at door and window for enrolment. Outside every recruiting office crowds of men and youths waited, leaning

> **Link**
>
> We will deal in more detail with Sassoon's prose writing in the next section on memoirs.

against walls, sitting upon the pavements, waited for long hours, waiting to the end of the day and returning next morning, without shelter, without food, many sick with hunger; men who had hurried up from the country, men who had thrown up jobs of every kind, clerks, shopmen, anxious only to serve England and 'teach those damned Germans a lesson'. Between them and this object they had discovered a perplexing barrier; an inattention. As Mr. Britling made his way by St. Martin's Church and across Trafalgar Square and marked the weary accumulation of this magnificently patriotic stuff, he had his first inkling of the imaginative insufficiency of the War Office that had been so suddenly called upon to organise Victory. He was to be more fully informed when he reached his club …

The prevailing topic in the smoking-room upstairs was the inability of the War Office to deal with the flood of recruits that was pouring in, and its hostility to any such volunteering as Mr. Britling had in mind. Quite a number of members wanted to volunteer; there was much talk of their fitness; 'I'm fifty-four,' said one, 'and I could do my twenty-five miles in marching kit far better than half those boys of nineteen.' Another was thirty-eight. 'I must hold the business together,' he said; 'but why anyhow shouldn't I learn to shoot and use a bayonet?' The personal pique of the rejected lent force to their criticisms of the recruiting and general organisation. 'The War Office has one incurable system,' said a big mine-owner. 'During peace time it runs all its home administration with men who will certainly be wanted at the front directly there is a war. Directly war comes, therefore, there is a shift all round, and a new untried man – usually a dug-out in an advanced state of decay – is stuck into the job. Chaos follows automatically. The War Office always has done this, and so far as one can see it always will. It seems incapable of realising that another man will be wanted until the first is taken away. Its imagination doesn't even run to that.'

Mr. Britling found a kindred spirit in Wilkins.

Wilkins was expounding his tremendous scheme for universal volunteering. Everybody was to be accepted. Everybody was to be assigned and registered and – badged.

'A brassard,' said Mr. Britling.

'It doesn't matter whether we really produce a fighting force or not,' said Wilkins. 'Everybody now is enthusiastic – and serious. Everybody is willing to put on some kind of uniform and submit to some sort of orders. And the thing to do is to catch them in the willing stage. Now is the time to get the country lined up and organised, ready to meet the internal stresses that are bound to come later. But there's no disposition whatever to welcome this universal offering. It's just as though this war was a treat to which only the very select friends of the War Office were to be admitted. And I don't admit that the national volunteers would be ineffective – even from a military point of view. There are plenty of fit men of our age, and men of proper age who are better employed at home – armament workers for example, and there are all the boys under the age. They may not be under the age before things are over …'

He was even prepared to plan uniforms.

'A brassard,' repeated Mr. Britling, 'and perhaps coloured strips on the revers of a coat.'

'Colours for the counties,' said Wilkins, 'and if there isn't coloured cloth to be got there's – red flannel. Anything is better than leaving the mass of the people to mob about …'

A momentary vision danced before Mr. Britling's eyes of red flannel petticoats being torn up in a rapid improvisation of soldiers to resist a sudden invasion. Passing washerwomen suddenly requisitioned. But one must not let oneself be laughed out of good intentions because of ridiculous accessories. The idea at any rate was the sound one …

The vision of what ought to be done shone brightly while Mr. Britling and Mr. Wilkins maintained it. But presently under discouraging reminders that there were no rifles, no instructors, and, above all, the open hostility of the established authorities, it faded again …

Afterwards in other conversations Mr. Britling reverted to more modest ambitions.

'Is there no clerical work, no minor administrative work, a man might be used for?' he asked.

'Any old dug-out,' said the man with the tin face, 'any old doddering Colonel Newcombe, is preferred to you in that matter …'

Mr. Britling emerged from his club about half-past three with his mind rather dishevelled and with his private determination to do something promptly for his country's needs blunted by a perplexing 'How?' His search for doors and ways where no doors and ways existed went on with a gathering sense of futility.

He had a ridiculous sense of pique at being left out, like a child shut out from a room in which a vitally interesting game is being played.

'After all, it is our war,' he said.

Fig. 1 *A recruiting poster designed to encourage men to enlist in the armed forces using guilt*

---

*From **Mr. Britling Sees It Through** by H.G. Wells*

Extract A (ii)

On August 3, 1914, I was a young schoolboy on my holidays, playing tennis in a set of mixed doubles. About five o'clock a paper-boy entered the tennis-club grounds with the Evening News. My male opponent, although he was serving, stopped his game for a minute and bought a paper.

'Hang the paper!' called I, indifferent to the fact that the Old World was falling about our ears and England's last day of peace was going down with the afternoon sun. 'Your service. Love – fifteen.'

'By Jove,' he cried, after scanning the paper, 'we're in!'

'What do you mean,' cried the girls, 'have the Germans declared war on us?'

'No. But we've sent an ultimatum to Germany which expires at twelve tonight. That means Britain will be in a state of war with Germany as from midnight.' The hand that held the paper trembled with excitement.

'How frightfully thrilling!' said one girl.

'How awful!' whispered the other.

'How ripping!' corrected I. 'Crash on with the game. Your service. Love – fifteen.'

Five days later it was decided that I should not return to school, but should go at once into the army. So it was that I never finished up in the correct style at Kensingstowe with an emotional last chapel, endless good wishes and a lump in my throat. I just didn't go back.

Instead, an influential friend, who knew the old Colonel of the 2nd Tenth East Cheshires, a territorial battalion of my grandfather's regiment, secured for me and, at my request, for Doe commissions in that unit.

So one day we two trusty and well-beloved subjects, flushed, very nervous, and clad in the most expensive khaki uniforms that

London could provide, took the train for the North to interview the Colonel of the 2nd Tenth. He was sitting at a littered writing-table, when we were shown in by a smart orderly. We saw a plump old territorial Colonel, grey-haired, grey-moustached, and kindly in face. His khaki jacket was brightened by the two South African medal ribbons; and we were so sadly fresh to things military as to wonder whether either was the V.C. We saluted with great smartness, and hoped we had made the movement correctly: for really we knew very little about it. I wasn't sure whether we ought to salute indoors; and Doe, having politely bared his fair head on entering the office, saluted without a cap. I blushed at my bad manners and surreptitiously removed mine. Not knowing what to do with my hands, I put them in my pockets. I knew that, if something didn't happen quickly, I should start giggling. Here in the presence of our new commanding officer I felt as I used to when I stood before the head master.

'Sit down,' beamed the C.O.

We sat down, crossed our legs, and tried to appear at our ease, and languid; as became officers.

'How old are you?' the Colonel asked Doe.

Doe hesitated, wondering whether to perjure himself and say 'Twenty.'

'Eighteen, sir,' he admitted, obviously ashamed.

'And you, Ray?'

'Eighteen, sir,' said I, feeling Doe's companion in guilt.

'Splendid, perfectly splendid!' replied the Colonel. 'Eighteen, by Jove! You've timed your lives wonderfully, my boys. To be eighteen in 1914 is to be the best thing in England. England's wealth used to consist in other things. Nowadays you boys are the richest thing she's got. She's solvent with you, and bankrupt without you. Eighteen, confoundit! It's a virtue to be your age, just as it's a crime to be mine. Now, look here' – the Colonel drew up his chair, as if he were going to get to business – 'look here. Eighteen years ago you were born for this day. Through the last eighteen years you've been educated for it. Your birth and breeding were given you that you might officer England's youth in this hour. And now you enter upon your inheritance. Just as this is the day in the history of the world so yours is the generation. No other generation has been called to such grand things, and to such crowded, glorious living. Any other generation at your age would be footling around, living a shallow existence in the valleys, or just beginning to climb a slope to higher things. But you' – here the Colonel tapped the writing-table with his forefinger – 'you, just because you've timed your lives aright, are going to be transferred straight to the mountain-tops. Well, I'm damned. Eighteen!'

I remember how his enthusiasm radiated from him and kindled a responsive excitement in me. I had entered his room a silly boy with no nobler thought than a thrill in the new adventure on which I had so suddenly embarked. But, as this fatherly old poet, touched by England's need and by the sight of two boys entering his room, so fresh and strong and ready for anything, broke into eloquence, I saw dimly the great ideas he was striving to express. I felt the brilliance of being alive in this big moment; the pride of youth and strength. I felt Aspiration surging in me and speeding up the action of my heart. I think I half hoped it would be my high lot to die on the battlefield.

*From **Tell England** by Ernest Raymond*

■ Questions

AO1: Developing an informed response to the text

■ Make notes about what is happening in each extract.

■ What does each extract tell us about the thoughts and feelings of those trying to recruit for war and of the attitudes of officials?

AO2: Understanding how structure, form and language shape meaning

■ Explore the narrative viewpoint in each extract – how appropriate is the choice each writer makes?

■ What do you notice about each writer's choice of language and its effect?

AO3: Exploring connections, comparisons and the interpretations of other readers

■ Compare the extracts in terms of subject matter and style.

■ Compare them to any other World War One literature you have read on the subject of recruitment.

■ How far do you think each extract has the purpose of celebrating the patriotic commitment of those who fought and died?

■ What do you think a 21st-century reader's response to such writing might be?

AO4: Understanding the significance and influence of contexts

■ What do you notice about the ways each writer is influenced by and uses the context of World War One?

■ Memoirs

In this section we concentrate on the many memoirs written after World War One. Many writers found this was the most effective way of organising their thoughts – and, as we saw in the previous section, several writers turned to memoirs, having felt some dissatisfaction with their efforts to write fiction. For the first few years after the war there was nothing, but then there was an outpouring of recollection.

Vera Brittain and female record keepers

Writing by male combatants was, of course the dominant genre, but it is worth noting the centrality of *Testament of Youth* by Vera Brittain (1933). Vera Brittain lost her brother and several of his friends, as well as her fiancé, in the war. Abandoning her plans to go to Oxford University, she also served as a VAD both in England and abroad. She kept a detailed diary, wrote and received copious letters and she drew on and included extracts from such writings – as well as from her own poetry – in her memoir. Extract C in Chapter 7 is taken from *Testament of Youth*; and the context question on the sample exam paper (see Chapter 8) is taken from a letter to her mother published in *Letters from a Lost Generation*, edited by Alan Bishop and Mark Bostridge (1998).

It is also worth dipping into *The Virago Book of Women and the Great War*, edited by Joyce Marlow (1999), in which there are contributions from women who took over the jobs of surgeons, nurses, foresters, censors, bus conductors, police constables, train drivers, bank clerks and munitions workers.

■ Did you know?

The VAD (Voluntary Aid Detachment) was a voluntary organisation providing auxiliary nursing services. During World War One, nurses were in short supply, and the VAD supplemented the work of registered nurses.

Male memoirs

From the ranks came books like Wyndham Lewis's *Blasting and Bombardiering* (1937). Lewis was a painter and novelist in the Royal Garrison Artillery. His book expresses anti-war sentiments in a contemptuous rather than in an angry way. He points out the stupidity of the war operations at a time when a second world war was approaching. This is a book packed with the visual detail that one might expect from an artist.

Frank Richards served as a private with Graves and Sassoon in the 2nd Battalion Royal Welch Fusiliers and wrote *Old Soldiers Never Die* (1933), a tough and humorous rather than a reflective memoir.

In *Sagittarius Rising* (1936), C.S. Lewis painted a vivid picture of the contrast between an indulged life on the ground and the daily encounter with death in the air.

And it is worth noting T.E. Lawrence's *Seven Pillars of Wisdom* (1935), which describes a different theatre of war, telling of his part in organising the revolt of the Arabs against the Turks and their German allies.

Other memoirs worth dipping into are Herbert Read's *In Retreat* (1925) and Richard Aldington's *Life for Life's Sake*.

Poets looking back

Three poets, who were infantry officers, served on and survived the Somme and wrote memoirs of note – Sassoon, Graves and Blunden.

Robert Graves's *Good-bye to All That* was published in 1929. This was not just the story of his war but a full-scale autobiography, full of fascinating anecdotes and reflecting his strong and unusual personality. Graves is not pro-war, but accepts his duty with stoic resignation. His approach to his war experiences is understated and detached. Critics have called this book a 'fictionalised autobiography', and, although Graves presents this book as 'autobiography', he is careful to point out the difference between the 'truthful' and the 'true':

> It was practically impossible (as well as forbidden) to keep a diary in any active trench-sector, or to send letters home which would be of any great post-War documentary value; and the more efficient the soldier the less time, of course, he took from his job to write about it. Great latitude should therefore be allowed to a soldier who has since got his facts or dates mixed. I would even paradoxically say that the memoirs of a man who went through some of the worst experiences of trench warfare are not truthful if they do not contain a high proportion of falsities.

Sassoon's journey from fiction to memoir is particularly interesting. In 1928 he published *Memoirs of a Fox-Hunting Man*, a book that paints an idyllic picture of pre-war rural English life. The main character is George Sherston, who joins up in 1914. His army experiences are continued in *Memoirs of an Infantry Officer** which appeared in 1930. George is not Siegfried, but the writer is clearly drawing on his own war experiences. The book goes on to describe the Sherston/Sassoon protest against the continuation of the war and ends with his arrival at Craiglockhart Hospital ('Slateford' in the book). In the final volume of the trilogy, *Sherston's Progress* (1936), Sassoon tells of the time at Craiglockhart, the relationship with W.H.R. Rivers and his return to the Front. Even in his 'straight' memoir, *Siegfried's Journey* (1945), Sassoon shows that there is a fine line between the truth and being what Graves called 'truthful, not true'. Towards the end of this book, Sassoon writes:

It needs no pointing out that there is an essential disparity between being alive and memorizing about it long afterwards. But the recorder of his vanished self must also bear this in mind, that his passage through time was a confused experiment, and that external circumstances had yet to become static and solidly discernible … In relation to his surroundings my younger self seemed to be watching a play performed in a language of which he couldn't understand more than an occasional word. His apprehensions of the contemporary scene were blinkered, out of focus, and amorphous as the imagery of a dream. I have felt that throughout the journey described in this book he was like someone driving a motor-car on a foggy night, only able to see a few yards in front of him. Nevertheless I have contrived to reconstruct an outline which represents everything as though it had been arranged for him beforehand.

The third officer poet was Blunden, who published *Undertones of War* in 1928. This is a memoir that concentrates on Blunden's experiences as a very young subaltern on the Somme. It includes some of his poetry. It is a generally accepted view that this memoir 'presents' experiences but does not comment on them. There follows an extract from this memoir as well as an extract from a memoir *(World Without End)* written by Helen Thomas, the wife of the poet Edward Thomas. Blunden is describing an experience in the trenches; Thomas, using the pseudonyms of David and Jenny, describes the night before her husband leaves to go back to the Front. He was killed in the Battle of Arras in 1917.

Extract B (i)

The communication trench was one of the longest we ever used, and in many places it was bricked, sides and floor. It ended in a singular front line, approached by too many boyaux, known by their numbers; a front line not unhappily sited, but dominated by the enemy's higher ground, on which rose Auchy's crowding red roofs. Our company's notch of this front line was a deep trench, passing every twenty or thirty yards under roofs or iron rails or duckboards covered with sandbags. And this trench had been kept elegantly clean. On the wrong side of it, their mouths facing the German line, were several deep dug-outs; forward from it reached several saps, chalky grooves which were by no means so tidy. And, not without their awe to the unaccustomed, there were mine-shafts in the line, mostly with wooden barriers and notices excluding infantry. 'Keep Out. This Means You,' was seen here.

The reason for the overhead coverings did not long keep me in suspense. It was my turn of trench watch, one grey morning; I walked to our left-hand post, and talked to our sentry there, when whiz-crunch, whiz-crunch, two small trench mortar shells of the kind called 'pine-apples' fell on the covering above us, broke it half down and strewed the place with fragments. The immediateness of these arrivals annulled fear. Taking my meditative way along to the other extremity of our trench, I was genially desired by Corporal Worley to take cocoa with him; he was just bringing it to the boil over some shreds of sandbag and tallow candle. Scarcely had I grasped the friendly mug when a rifle-grenade burst fizzing on the parapet behind me and another on the parados behind him; and we were unhit. Worley's courtesy and warm feeling went on, undiverted as though a butterfly or two had settled on a flower.

Fig. 2 *In the trenches*

The tunnellers who were so busy under the German line were men of stubborn determination, yet (by force of the unaccustomed) they hurried nervously along the trenches above ground to spend their long hours listening or mining. At one shaft they pumped air down with Brobdingnagian bellows. The squeaking noise may have given them away, or it may have been mere bad luck, when one morning a minenwefer smashed this entrance and the men working there. One was carried out past me, collapsing like a sack of potatoes, spouting blood at twenty places. Cambrin was beginning to terrify. Not far away from that shafthead, a young and cheerful lance-corporal of ours was making some tea as I passed one warm afternoon. I went along three firebays; one shell burst behind me; I saw its smoke faint out, and I thought all was as lucky as it should be. Soon a cry from that place recalled me; the shell had burst all wrong. Its butting impression was black and stinking in the parados where three minutes ago the lance-corporal's mess-tin was bubbling over a little flame. For him, how could the gobbets of blackening flesh, the earth-wall sotted with blood, with flesh, the eye under the duckboard, the pulpy bone be the only answer? At this moment, while we looked with intense fear at so strange a horror, the lance-corporal's brother came round the traverse.

He was sent to company headquarters in a kind of catalepsy. The bay had to be put right, and Sergeant Simmons, having helped himself and me to a share of rum, shovelled into the sandbag I held, not without self-protecting profanity, and an air of 'it's a lie; we're a lie.' Cambrin was beginning to terrify.

*From **Undertones of War** by Edmund Blunden*

Extract B (ii)

The last evening comes. The children have taken down the holly and mistletoe and ivy, and chopped up the little Christmas-tree to burn. And for a treat Elizabeth and Polly are to have their bath in front of the blazing fire. The big zinc bath is dragged in, and the children undress in high glee, and skip about naked in the warm room, which is soon filled with the sweet smell of the burning greenery. The berries pop, and the fir-tree makes fairy lace, and the holly crackles and roars. The two children get into the bath together, and David scrubs them in turn – they laughing, making the fire hiss with their splashing. The drawn curtains shut out the snow and the starless sky, and the deathly silence out there in the biting cold is forgotten in the noise and warmth of our little room. After the bath David reads to them. First of all he reads Shelley's The Question and Chevy Chase, and then for Polly a favourite Norse tale. They sit in their nightgowns listening gravely, and then, just before they kiss him good-night, while I stand by with the candle in my hand, he says:

'Remember while I am away to be kind. Be kind, first of all, to Mummy, and after that be kind to everyone and everything.' And they all assent together, and joyfully hug and kiss him, and he carries the two girls up, and drops each into her bed.

And we are left alone, unable to hide our agony, afraid to show it. Over supper we talk of the probable front he'll arrive at, of his fellow-officers, and of the unfinished portrait-etching that one of them has done of him and given to me. And we speak of the garden, and where this year he wants the potatoes to be, and he reminds me to put in the beans directly the snow disappears. 'If I'm not back in time you'd better get someone to help you with the digging,' he says. He reads me some of the poems he has written that I have not heard – the last one of all called Out in the Dark. And I venture to question one line, and he says, 'Oh no, it's right, Jenny, I'm sure it's right.' And I nod because I can't speak, and I try to smile at his assurance.

I sit and stare stupidly at his luggage by the wall, and his roll of bedding, kit-bag, and suit-case. He takes out his prismatic compass and explains it to me, but I cannot see, and when a tear drops on to it he just shuts it up and puts it away. Then he says, as he takes a book out of his pocket, 'You see, your Shakespeare's Sonnets is already where it will always be. Shall I read you some?' He reads one or two to me. His face is grey and his mouth trembles, but his voice is quiet and steady. And soon I slip to the floor and sit between his knees, and while he reads his hand falls over my shoulder and I hold it with mine.

'Shall I undress you by this lovely fire and carry you upstairs in my khaki overcoat?' So he undoes my things, and I slip out of them; then he takes the pins out of my hair, and we laugh at ourselves for behaving as we so often do, like young lovers. 'We have never become a proper Darby and Joan, have we?'

*From **World Without End** by Helen Thomas*

Questions

AO1: Developing an informed response to the text
- What events and thoughts and feelings are described in each extract?
- How do you, the reader, respond to each extract?

AO2: Understanding how structure, form and language shape meaning
- How does each writer use the narrative viewpoint to convey ideas, thoughts and feelings?
- Explore the choices of language made by each author. What is their effect?

AO3: Exploring connections, comparisons and the interpretations of other readers
- Compare the extracts in terms of circumstance, tone and techniques used.
- What connections can you make between each extract and your wider reading?
- A critic called *Undertones of War* an 'undramatic' book and talked of Blunden's 'studied reticence'. How far can you apply these descriptions to each of the extracts?

AO4: Understanding the significance and influence of contexts
- Compare the ways the writers use the context of World War One in their writing.

■ 20th-century female fiction writers

Beware stereotypes!

World War One literature is a male-dominated literature, but there are significant texts by female writers at all points of the 20th century. What is more, in terms of the war years, we need to question the stereotype of the 'little woman' sitting waiting and grieving, since we have already noted that many women moved into new roles. Women may not have been in the trenches, but they were gaining experience and greater freedom.

You will need to look in the literature for signs of the obvious tensions between home and the Front, and between male and female roles.

Texts through time

One of earliest texts showing the anxiety of women waiting for the return of a shell-shocked soldier is *The Return of the Soldier*⋆ by Rebecca West (1918). The novels of Virginia Woolf – *Jacob's Room* and *Mrs Dalloway* – show her preoccupation with the war.

We That Were Young by Irene Rathbone (1932) provided one of the fullest accounts of lives of women during war as YMCA volunteers, VADs and munitions workers. Its central relationship between a woman and her brother invites comparison with Vera Brittain.

Not So Quiet⋆ by Helen Zenna Smith appeared in 1930. This book is based on the wartime diaries of a female ambulance driver.

Bid Me to Live by H.D. was published in 1960, but had been started in 1918. H.D. was an American poet living in London who married Richard Aldington. Her book paints a picture of London life during the years 1914–18 and traces the collapse of her marriage. It can be compared with Aldington's own account of the story in *Death of a Hero*.

Clearly Susan Hill relied on her own research and powers of imaginative reconstruction to write *Strange Meeting*⋆ in 1971. The book has a strong male friendship under the stress of the front at its heart; it takes its title from Owen's poem.

In the 1990s, Pat Barker wrote the Regeneration trilogy⋆. *Regeneration*⋆ (1991), set in 1917, concerns Siegfried Sassoon, Dr Rivers, victims of shell shock and the issue of their 'regeneration'. *The Eye in the Door*⋆ (1993) and *The Ghost Road*⋆ (1995) extend the scope of the trilogy by moving to London and the Front, as well as Craiglockhart. Barker presents a full range of views on the war, an extensive selection of characters from different social classes, and deals with homosexuality and psychotherapy in a way that earlier writers could not.

Collections

To gain an impression of the range and variety of women's writing and experiences, you might like to look through *Women's Writing on the First World War* edited by Agnès Cardinal, Dorothy Goldman and Judith Hattaway (1999). You will find both fiction and non-fiction writing from the years 1914 to 1930.

The following extract is taken from a short story called *The Beach*, written by Mary Borden during the war and published in her book *The Forbidden Zone* – a collection of sketches, short stories and poems based on her nursing experiences – in 1929. Mary Borden was a wealthy American who settled in Britain and was well-known on the pre-war literary scene. She counted George Bernard Shaw, Wyndham Lewis and Ford Madox Ford among her friends. Her first husband, Captain Turner, was busy with counter-espionage work, so she turned to the equipping of a mobile hospital which was attached to the French army at the Front. She stayed with it throughout the war.

Extract C

The man wriggled and hitched himself clumsily up in his chair; an ugly grimace pulled his pale face to one side. He dared not look down over the arm of his wheel chair at the bright head of the woman sitting beside him. Her hair burned in the sunlight; her cheeks were pink. He stole a timid, furtive look. Yes, she was as beautiful as a child. She was perfectly lovely. A groan escaped him, or was it only a sigh?

She looked up quickly. 'What is it, darling? Are you in pain? Are you tired? Shall we go back?' Her voice sounded in the immense quiet of the beach like a cricket chirping, but the word 'darling' went on sounding and sounding like a little hollow bell while she searched his features, trying to find his old face, the one she knew, trying to work a magic on him, remove and replace the sunken eyes, the pinched nose, the bloodless wry mouth. 'He's not a stranger,' she said to herself. 'He's not.' And she heard the faint mocking echo, 'Darling, darling', ringing far away as if a bell-buoy out on the water were saying 'Darling, darling', to make the little waves laugh.

'It's only my foot, my left foot. Funny, isn't it, that it goes on throbbing. They cut it off two months ago.' He jerked a hand backward. 'It's damn queer when you think of it. The old foot begins the old game, then I look down and it's not there any more, and I'm fooled again.' He laughed. His laughter was such a tiny sound in the great murmur of the morning that it might have been a sand-fly laughing. He was thinking, 'What will become of us? She is young and healthy. She is as beautiful as a child. What shall we do about it?' And looking into her eyes he saw the same question, 'What shall we do?' and looked quickly away again. So did she.

She looked past him at the row of ugly villas above the beach. Narrow houses, each like a chimney, tightly wedged together, wedges of cheap brick and plaster with battered wooden balconies. They were new and shabby and derelict. All had their shutters up. All the doors were bolted. How stuffy it must be in those deserted villas, in all those abandoned bedrooms and kitchens and parlours. Probably there were sand-shoes and bathing dresses and old towels and saucepans and blankets rotting inside them with the sand drifting in. Probably the window panes behind the shutters were broken and the mirrors cracked. Perhaps when the aeroplanes dropped bombs on the town, pictures fell down and mirrors and the china in the dark china closets cracked inside these pleasure houses. Who had built them?

'Cowards built them,' he said in his new bitter, rasping voice, the voice of a peevish, irritable sandfly. 'Built them to make love in, to cuddle in, to sleep in, hide in. Now they're empty. The

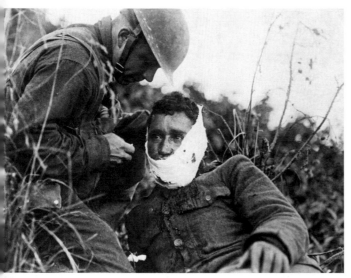

Fig. 3 *Many soliders returned from the war seriously wounded Their experiences are recorded in memoirs and echoed in fiction*

blighters have left them to rot there. Rotten, I call it, leaving the swanky plage to go to the bad like that, just because there's a war on. A little jazz now and a baccarat table would make all the difference, wouldn't it? It would cheer us up. You'd dance and I'd have a go at the tables. That's the casino over there, that big thing; that's not empty, that's crowded, but I don't advise you to go there. I don't think you'd like it. It's not your kind of a crowd. It's all right for me, but not for you. No, it wouldn't do for you – not even on a gala night.

'They've a gala night in our casino whenever there's a battle. Funny sort of place. You should watch the motors drive up then. The rush begins about ten in the evening and goes on till morning. Quite like Deauville the night of the Grand Prix. You never saw such a crowd. They all rush there from the front, you know – the way they do from the race-course – though, to be sure, it is not quite the real thing – not really a smart crowd. No, not precisely, though the wasters in Deauville weren't much to look at, were they? Still, our crowd here aren't precisely wasters. Gamblers, of course, down and outs, wrecks – all gone to pieces, parts of 'em missing, you know, tops of their heads gone, or one of their legs. When they take their places at the tables, the croupiers – that is to say, the doctors – look them over. Come closer, I'll whisper it. Some of them have no faces.'

'Darling, don't,' She covered her own face, closed her ears to his tiny voice and listened desperately with all her minute will to the large tranquil murmur of the sea. 'Darling, darling', far out the bell-buoy was sounding.

'Bless you,' said the tin, sharp, exasperated sandfly voice beside her. 'Little things like that don't keep us away. If we can't walk in we get carried in. All that's needed is a ticket. It's tied to you like a luggage label. It has your name on it in case you don't remember your name. You needn't have a face, but a ticket you must have to get into our casino.'

'Stop, darling – darling, stop!'

*From **The Beach** by Mary Borden*

■ Questions

AO1: Developing an informed response to the text

■ What do you notice about the relationship between the two people described here?

■ What thoughts and feelings are expressed?

AO2: Understanding how structure, form and language shape meaning

■ Comment on the writer's choice of narrative viewpoint.

■ Explore the writer's use of contrast.

■ How does the writer use the setting?

■ What is the effect of the repetition?

AO3: Exploring connections, comparisons and the interpretations of other readers

■ Compare this extract with other writing about the war by female writers.

■ How do you respond to the criticism that women's writing tends to ignore the harsh realities of war? How far do you think that criticism applies to this extract?

AO4: Understanding the significance and influence of contexts

■ How does Borden use the context of World War One in her story?

■ Writing from other countries

It is interesting to look at literature from other countries involved in World War One and to compare it with our own. What first strikes one is the sheer volume of our own World War One literature, as well as the fact that we are still 'writing the war'. Other countries do not seem to share our continued preoccupation; nor are they so prolific. You may wish to ask yourself why it is that World War One remains such a subject of interest for British writers almost a century later.

France

The earliest of these writings is *Le Feu* (*Under Fire*) by the French writer Henri Barbusse. He wrote originally in serial form during 1916–17. His aim was to show the suffering, the horror and a picture of a world changed beyond recognition so that another war would never happen. In his book *Sites of Memory, Sites of Mourning* (1995), Jay Winter writes:

> Le Feu offered a message of hope. This is what helped to give his book its massive appeal and power. It spoke to the bereaved as much as to the soldiers with whom Barbusse had served.

One teacher from the Ardèche, aged 20, lost her husband in the war. She wrote to Barbusse to thank him for his book and for his message of hope. She 'took courage to think that those who died did not die in vain – if the present cataclysm produces a modification of human destiny'. 'One can't remake life', Barbusse mused, 'but one can avoid death' in future. It was this task, the avoidance of another dreadful war, which Barbusse was to make his life's work.

Germany

Two German books published in 1929 were sharply contrasting. Erich Maria Remarque's novel *Im Westen Nichts Neues (All Quiet on the Western Front)* is generally seen as having much in common with the English writing on the war, emphasising the pity, rather than the anger. It takes a group of friends who enlisted together and are increasingly drawn together as they are cut off from home at the Front. In his book *English Literature Between the Wars* (1948), Ifor Evans, a literary historian, accuses the book of being a 'crude and sentimental' volume with a strain that is almost hysterical. He was also of the opinion that the writing of Aldington and Hemingway was more genuinely 'realistic' and 'authentic' than that of Remarque. The other book, the memoir *In Stahlgewittern (Storm of Steel)* by Ernst Junger, paints war as an ennobling experience and demonstrates a remarkable enthusiasm for war. Bernard Bergonzi in his book *Heroes' Twilight* (1965) suggests that the book has the subject matter of Owen and Sassoon with the patriotic attitudes of Brooke and Grenfell. The book ends with the following words:

> Though force without and barbarity within conglomerate in sombre clouds, yet so long as the blade of a sword will strike a spark in the right way it may be said: Germany lives and Germans shall never go under!

America

Anti-war novels were published in the 1920s by three American writers – John Dos Passos's *Three Soldiers* in 1921, e.e. cummings's *The Enormous Room* in 1922, and Ernest Hemingway's *A Farewell to Arms* in 1929. Generally, they are noted for their notes of protest and disillusion, which are more extreme than those of the English writers.

Recent

More recently (1998) the French novelist Marc Dugain published *La Chambre des Officiers (The Officers' Ward)*, a short novel that traces the story of Lieutenant Adrien F., who is injured in the first days of shooting in 1914, and who spends the next five years of his life in a closed ward, without mirrors, specially reserved for officers who have lost their faces.

Read the following extracts carefully, then do the activities. The first extract is taken from *Under Fire (Le Feu)* by Henri Barbusse, the second from *All Quiet on the Western Front (Im Westen Nichts Neues)* by Erich Maria Remarque. In both extracts, the soldiers reflect on the gulf between combatants and non-combatants.

Extract D (i)

Then he who spoke sorrowfully, like a bell, said, 'It'll be no good telling about it, eh? They wouldn't believe you; not out of malice or through liking to pull your leg, but because they couldn't. When you say to 'em later, if you live to say it, "We were on a night job and we got shelled and we were very nearly drowned in mud," they'll say "Ah!" And p'rhaps they'll say, "You didn't have a very spicy time on the job."' And that's all. No one can know it. Only us.'

'No, not even us, not even us!' some one cried.

'That's what I say, too. We shall forget – we're forgetting already, my boy!'

'We've seen too much to remember.'

'And everything we've seen was too much. We're not made to hold it all. It takes its bloody hook in all directions. We're too little to hold it.'

'You're right, we shall forget! Not only the length of the big misery, which can't be reckoned, as you say, ever since the beginning, but the marches that turn up the ground and turn it again, lacerating your feet and wearing out your bones under a load that seems to grow bigger in the sky, the exhaustion until you don't know your own name any more, the tramping and the inaction that grind you, the digging jobs that exceed your strength, the endless vigils when you fight against sleep and watch for the enemy who is everywhere in the night, the pillows of dung and lice – we shall forget not only those, but even the foul wounds of shells and machine-guns, the mines, the gas, and the counter-attacks. At those moments you're full of the excitement of reality, and you've some satisfaction. But all that wears off and goes away, you don't know how and you don't know where, and there's only the names left, only the words of it, like in a dispatch.'

'That's true what he says,' remarks a man, without moving his head in its pillory of mud. 'When I was on leave, I found I'd already jolly well forgotten what happened to me before. There were some letters from me that I read over again just as if they were a book I was opening. And yet in spite of that, I've forgotten also all the pain I've had in the war. We're forgetting machines. Men are things that think a little but chiefly forget. That's what we are.'

'Then neither the other side nor us'll remember! So much misery all wasted!'

This thought increased the abasement of these beings on the shore of the flood, like news of a great disaster, and humiliated them still more.

'Ah, if one did remember!' cried some one.

'If we remembered,' said another, 'there wouldn't be any more war.'

A third added grandly, 'Yes, if we remembered, war would be less useless than it is.'

But suddenly one of the prone survivors rose to his knees, dark as a great bat ensnared, and as the mud dripped from his waving arms, he cried in a hollow voice, 'There must be no more war after this!'

*From **Under Fire (Le Feu)** by Henri Barbusse*

Extract D (ii)

I imagined leave would be different from this. Indeed, it was different a year ago. It is I of course that have changed in the interval. There lies a gulf between that time and today. At that time I still knew nothing about the war, we had only been in quiet sectors. But now I see that I have been crushed without knowing it. I find I do not belong here any more, it is a foreign world. Some of these people ask questions, some ask no questions, but one can see that the latter are proud of themselves for their silence; they often say with a wise air that these things cannot be talked about. They plume themselves on it.

I prefer to be alone, so that no one troubles me. For they all come back to the same thing, how badly it goes and how well it goes; one thinks it is this way, another that; and yet they are always absorbed in the things that go to make up their existence. Formerly I lived in just the same way myself, but now I feel no contact here.

They talk too much for me. They have worries, aims, desires, that I cannot comprehend. I often sit with one of them in the little beer garden and try to explain to him that this is really the only thing: just to sit quietly like this. They understand of course, they agree, they may even feel it so too, but only with words, only with words, yes, that is it – they feel it, but always with only half of themselves, the rest of their being is taken up with other things, they are so divided in themselves that none feels it with his whole essence; I cannot even say myself exactly what I mean.

When I see them here, in their rooms, in their offices, about their occupations, I feel an irresistible attraction in it, I would like to be here too and forget the war; but also it repels me, it is so narrow, how can that fill a man's life, he ought to smash it to bits; how can they do it, while out at the front the splinters are whining over the shell-holes and the star-shells go up, the wounded are carried back on waterproof sheets and comrades crouch in the trenches. – They are different men here, men I cannot properly understand, whom I envy and despise.

*From **All Quiet on the Western Front (Im Westen Nichts Neues)** by Erich Maria Remarque*

■ Questions

AO1: Developing an informed response to the text

- What is the experience of the soldiers here?
- What are their thoughts and feelings?
- What do they have to say about the gap between home and the Front?

AO2: Understanding how structure, form and language shape meaning

- How effective is the writer's use of narrative viewpoint?
- Explore the use of contrast in each extract.
- What do you notice about the choices of language each writer makes?

AO3: Exploring connections, comparisons and the interpretations of other readers

- Compare the differences in approach of the two writers.
- What connections can you make with other texts from your wider reading?
- How far do you agree with the critical opinion that the Remarque book was written more in pity than anger?
- How far can you apply this assessment to each of these texts?

AO4: Understanding the significance and influence of contexts

- Explore the ways each of these writers uses the context of World War One.

■ 21st-century writers

The war continues to fascinate and provide raw material for British writers in the present century. One of these books – *A Long Long Way** by Sebastian Barry (2005) – is dealt with in Chapter 3, where it appears on the list of the ten texts. This novel is mostly set on the Western Front between 1914 and 1918, and draws on Barry's own family's history to tell the story of Private Willie Dunne's experiences in the Royal Dublin Fusiliers.

In the same year, Ben Elton published *The First Casualty,* a detective story that spans both the Home and the Western Front. A retired detective is asked to go to France to secure a conviction for the murder of a famous officer poet.

The book that we are going to concentrate on in this section, however, is a novel by Adam Thorpe called *Nineteen Twenty-One* (2001). The focus here is obviously on the aftermath of war, as a young man who missed the war tries to write the first great novel of the war. He goes on a tour of the battlefields which are still being cleared, and in the extract that follows he has become separated from the rest of his coach party.

Read it carefully and then answer the questions which follow.

Extract E

Better to have come in the winter, in really foul wet weather. The ground wanting you inside it.

Now the ground rebuffed you, sent dust up. There was a soldier's button stuck in it, as if the earth had been officially stamped. In fact, the more he looked, the more he saw, as with stars at night – glinting metallic bits and bobs, more and more of them. He might have been walking the high-water marge of a beach, but here everything was cemented in. Just where it had fallen into the prehistoric mire, just where men had lurched in raw cold through fog and soddenness – oh, that was quite impossible to imagine now!

He thought he saw a set of dentures, but it was only a part of a gas-rattle. A pilchard jar here, the edge of a tarpaulin there, as stiff as concrete. Another pilchard jar, with gobbets of something in it. The working parts of something giant, a howitzer perhaps, scattered like a diagram. Picket-irons to catch the foot on, webbing, eyeless goggles. The liquid world had frozen it all in.

He must come back here at night, he realised. For the scale of it, in the darkness.

He arrived at the point where he had seen the others pause. Beyond the tumbled-in trench, crossed by a couple of planks, he saw a sign with heavy Gothic lettering, very weathered, and scores of rusty iron crosses at all angles, their long shadows broken up by clumps of waving yarrow. The gold of the early evening glowed in there, caught by the neglect.

A German cemetery. Purely German.

A group of charred trees stood in the middle, their bark peeling off and the wood very white underneath, but otherwise intact and leafy. He crossed the planks and entered the cemetery, staying by the first of the crosses. Of course it was important to him to see the purely German side. The crosses immediately around him were wooden, already bleached and split. The careful, signboard lettering on the cracker-shaped cross-pieces – that was touching: Sold. Heinz Schumacher, Sold. Willy Stramm … Others illegible, vanished. Why had the guide not entered the German cemetery? What had she said about it? Had she said, 'Rejoice – there's a good few killed …'?

A figure rose from one of the iron crosses a few yards away – it made him jump.

It was a woman, not a decaying soldier. She had been kneeling; the evening light and the high flowering yarrow had disguised her. He felt somewhat embarrassed, as if he ought to have a better reason for being here. He stood uncertainly, holding his hat in front of him, giving the briefest of nods. He was not even sure she had seen him, since her full mourning included a veil: as well nod at the Sphinx, for she stood very still, head a little inclined towards the graves, her long, heavy skirt emerging from a short jacket and making her look leaden, really weighted by grief.

He wandered about discreetly, eyes fumbling over the stark, solid ironwork, over the alien names. Hans, Karl, Friedrich, Siegfried. The big German fair-haired boys under their iron swords. A few had rusty helmets propped on their crosses; meditative, they looked. Or abashed. He felt uneasy, standing among them. Genuinely uneasy, as if he had come into the enemy. It was the woman who made him feel this, watching almost closely. Though when he looked up, she was turned away slightly, not watching him at all.

He felt definitely that he should be out of the place. He had perhaps ruined it for her – the communion with the loved one. A bright patch of cloth flowers lay against one of the end crosses a few rows up. 'Weep, maiden, weep here o'er the tomb of Love' – he knew a smattering of Goethe's lines, not even a whole poem, and nothing in German. And that line of Goethe's was wholly out of place, here. Death here was not apparent, it was as stolid as iron. Love is never lifeless, not really, it can be revived by the slightest trifle – Goethe was quite right. But death!

The trees rattled their dry leaves – there were leaves already fallen, caught in the scented yarrow. Then a familiar bark of motor horn. The coach, a dark lump in the distance. Then another, crude: they were waiting for him. He was irritated, suddenly, by this impatience, this crude disturbing of the gravity of the place.

*From **Nineteen Twenty-One** by Adam Thorpe*

Fig. 4 *A German war cemetery*

■ Questions

AO1: Developing an informed response to the text

- ■ How do you respond to the character in this extract?
- ■ What do you learn about the landscape?
- ■ What do you make of the literary reference?

AO2: Understanding how structure, form and language shape meaning

- ■ Explore the choice of narrative viewpoint.
- ■ Examine the use of detail and description and its effects.
- ■ What use does Thorpe make of contrast, and why?

AO3: Exploring the connections, comparisons and the interpretations of other readers

- ■ What connections can you make between this extract and other texts in your wider reading? Think of writing that explores attitudes towards or meeting with the enemy.
- ■ A critical review of this book spoke of its 'dark and haunted' quality. How do you respond to this?

AO4: Understanding the significance and influence of contexts

- ■ Explore the ways the writer has used the context of World War One in this extract.

💡 ⓘ 🔍 *Summary*

In this chapter we have surveyed prose writing about World War One from the time of the war to the present day. As you keep a record of your reading, you will need to explore the ways different writers approach the **shared context**, and ask yourself the following questions:

- ■ What part does an interest in landscape play in the writing?
- ■ How dominant is the interest in relationships?
- ■ What are the writers' attitudes to war?
- ■ Is the writer describing 'real' experience?
- ■ Or is the writer shaping an imaginative reconstruction?
- ■ How far has the gender of the writer influenced the writing?
- ■ How has the time of composition influenced the writing?

6 Tackling wider reading in drama

Introduction

In the previous two chapters we have covered wider reading in poetry and prose. Now we turn to wider reading in drama.

When you attempt the context question in the AS examination, your answer should include some relevant references to plays you have studied, so it is important that you are familiar with a range of World War One plays. As well as studying plays in printed form, you will find it helpful to experience them in performance. You should try to see some of these plays live on stage – or at least on film or DVD.

In this chapter we look in detail at **seven extracts** from **five** different plays. We will look at them chronologically, noting the ways the writing and performing contexts change through the 20th and into the 21st century.

We are going to look at **four time periods:**

1 drama during the war
2 drama in the years after the war
3 drama after 1945
4 drama from the 1980s to the present day.

Questions to consider as you read

You will notice that there are distinct differences between the relatively small **amount** of drama about World War One and the outpouring of prose and poetry. The few plays that there are also attract significantly less critical attention. Most people, if asked to identify a World War One play, might name *Journey's End* or *Oh! What a Lovely War*, but the record is indeed more complex that this. You will need to consider why so few soldiers turned their World War One experience into plays.

Interestingly, over the last few years there has been a significant production of *Journey's End* as well as several attempts to find and revive less well-known plays. (Two's Company Theatre Company, for example, has produced several unknown World War One plays each season in recent years.)

Some background: the theatre before World War One

After 1737, when the Walpole government passed a stage censorship law, most serious authors had abandoned the theatre for the comparative freedom of prose fiction and poetry writing. The early Victorian repertoire consisted mainly of **melodramas**, pantomimes and 'improved' versions of Shakespeare (actor managers removed the dirty jokes, added extra characters and rewrote tragedies with happy endings!). The 1848 Theatres' Act increased government control over the stage so much that the mid-Victorian theatre tended to rely on imported French **farces** and adaptations of popular novels (Dickens was a particular favourite with audiences).

It was not until the final decades of the 19th century that drama began to be considered as serious literature. Writers including Ibsen, Wilde and Shaw attracted a new, educated, middle-class audience as fashionable theatres mounted productions of social drama and sophisticated **satire**. For the working classes, there were music halls: cheap, popular variety theatres where the tradition of melodrama lived on – until the arrival of the silent movies.

It is worth noting the emergence of suffrage drama – plays about 'the vote' and with a focus on issues of gender roles. For example, Cicely Hamilton's *Diana of Dobson's* appeared in 1908, George Bernard Shaw's *Press Cuttings* in 1910, and Charlotte Gilman's *Three Women* in 1912. However, World War One brought the suffrage theatre as well as the suffragette campaign to a halt.

🎭 💡 Drama during World War One

The state of the theatre during the war years was summed up by W.A. Darlington, a theatre reviewer for the *Daily Telegraph*, when he wrote in 1919, after serving in the war: 'the art of theatre dropped dead when war was declared'.

Audiences demanded escapist productions such as revues, farces and musicals. The most popular farce during the war was *A Little Bit of Fluff* by W.E. Ellis, with 1,241 performances. Escapist it was, and generally regarded as 'a good night out' by an audience that included many soldiers. The smash hit of the period was Asche's *Chu Chin Chow*, with 2,235 performances. This was the story of Ali Baba and the 40 thieves. Sets and costumes were opulent and there was singing, wit and nudity!

Some plays that did focus on the times – *The Man Who Stayed at Home* and *General Post* – were no more than patriotic propaganda, offering more proof of the audience's resistance to **social realism**.

Other, serious plays which tried to expose the truth were banned. For example, George Bernard Shaw lost many battles against the censor. He was strongly opposed to jingoism and the glorifying of the war. His play *O'Flaherty VC* was a devastating attack on the war and on Britain's consideration of conscription in Ireland. In the preface to the play he considers the absurdity of Britain's signing up Irish men loyal to Ireland, and mostly Roman Catholic, at the same time as regarding them as heretics and rebels. There was no chance that this play would be performed in England. Shaw continued to write plays with a more general anti-war message.

Drinkwater's play, $X = O$, was performed in 1917, but its setting in the Trojan War veiled its pacifist message which stressed the futility of war.

The slaughter of millions in the trenches was too shocking and too close to the audience to work as 'entertainment'. The theatre during the war was no place to present the horror and filth of trenches with anything like accuracy and truth. In time, as you will see from the later extracts, this would not be such a problem.

The extract that follows is taken from a play called *Black 'ell* by Miles Malleson. In this play, the parents of a soldier in France learn from a newspaper that he has been awarded a DSO for killing six of the enemy and that he is coming home that morning. While they rush off to the station, the son arrives at the house, and it is at this point that the light-hearted tone of the play changes. Harold, the son, is haunted by the enemies he has killed and is re-living the deaths with horror.

Both this and Malleson's other play, *D Company*, were confiscated by the War Office and Scotland Yard. A cabinet minister called the play 'a deliberate calumny of the British soldier'. The play was not republished until 1925. Malleson himself said 'to write a deliberate calumny of the British soldier was the last thing I wanted to do, yet the book was called that by a cabinet minister who had not read it'.

Extract A

In this scene, Harold Gould has just returned on leave to learn that he has been awarded a medal for distinguished service. Here we see not only his own reaction to the news, but also the reactions of his parents, of his girlfriend Jean, and of his uncle, the Colonel.

Harold (*Almost to himself.*) No... it isn't true ... It isn't true. (*he stares at the little group; and hypnotised as **Jean** was, they wait in silence. He is evidently striving again with the past.*) ... There were six in it when I started, and it was empty when he came... If I could remember ... O, my Christ! If it is true ... and they want to reward me for it. (*He talks horribly in the air.*) I won't take it ... I won't touch it ... You know I won't, don't you? (*He sinks into a chair, covering his face with his hands.*) O, my Christ!

Mr. Gould Hullo!

Mrs. Gould What is it?

Jean He's been telling me – it isn't a bit like we expected ... he's been telling me about the man he killed.

Colonel It's all right, people; they're often like that at first ... shock, you know – nerves ... he'll be all right in a day or two.

(***Harold** has not raised his head from his hands, and **Mr. Gould**, going to him, pats him gently and kindly on the shoulder.*)

Mr. Gould There, there, there; my dear old chap; we understand ... of course, we do ... one or two good breakfasts at home, a few nights in your own comfortable bed, and a dinner with me at the Club, eh? ... you'll be as right as rain. (*No answer.*) Come along, old man, pull yourself together. (*No answer.*) It sounds strange, here in my own house, telling the soldier who's been facing death for us for nearly a year to 'pull himself together'.

Harold (*Suddenly looking up.*) It isn't a soldier's job to get killed ... it's his job to kill.

Mr. Gould (*Momentarily nonplussed.*) Yes ... but –

Harold You know it isn't them so much ... or even him ... it's her, waiting there ... coming back to Jean makes you realise.

Mr. Gould Oh, come, come, come! ... you've killed your men, we know; but it was in fair fight.

Harold Fair fight!

Mr. Gould Well, if it wasn't fair fight, it wasn't you that was fighting foul ... We know that ... I shouldn't let myself be weak.

Harold Fair fight! If you only knew what it means ... All of it ... all fighting's foul!

Mr. Gould Oh, come – that's rather a queer view! (*He tries a little joviality.*) We get quite enough of that sort of thing from the cranks at home. We can't do with any sentimentalism, you know, from the men who are doing the work.

Harold Fair fight!

(*He is evidently on the verge of breaking down completely. **The Colonel**, who is not a man of words, has taken up his position with his back to the fireplace; **Mrs. Gould** and **Jean** can only watch and listen. When **Mr. Gould** speaks again, he is entirely serious.*)

Mr. Gould Come, old man, I want you to listen to me, quietly… are you listening? (*Harold nods assent.*) … Look here … if a criminal was to come into this room and attack me, or your mother, or Jean, you'd be the first to protect us … Eh? … of course you would. Well, that's what you've been doing … and you wouldn't be so upset if you happened to damage the blackguard in the process … of course you wouldn't … my dear old chap, nobody wanted this war … but if you're attacked you've got to defend yourself … That's all it is … it's perfectly simple … but, by Jove! We are proud of you, and we are thankful to you for the way you've been protecting your home, and your country, and all that she stands for.

Harold D'you know when I heard all that last? … all of it almost … in their trenches. (*He has risen in a passionate, nervous excitement.*) I was lying there all night, quite close, and I heard them talking, just like our chaps do sometimes – laughing and joking about all the things they're going through, and knowing they've got to climb out in the morning and don't stand a dog's chance of being alive – not death itself simply, but bits of you smashed up, and you lie and roll about; you can hear them crying out all over the place – and the night before they wait … and make fun … and they know all the time – it's just in the early morning, when it gets a bit colder and the light begins to come in the sky, waiting – my God! They are fine, all of 'em … d'you think they'd do that to each other, month after month, if they didn't both think they were right and the others wrong, and they were protecting something? It's all a bloody muddle!

Mr. Gould Harold!!

Further reading/viewing

- John Drinkwater, *X = 0 (1917)*
- Miles Malleson, *D Company (1916)*
- George Bernard Shaw, *O'Flaherty VC (1915)*
- Marie Leneru, *La Paix (1918)* French play debating pacifism and militarism
- Gertrude Stein, *Please Do Not Suffer* (1916)
- Marion Craig Wentworth, *War Brides* (1915) – feminist anti-war play
- Alice Dunbar Wilson, *Mine Eyes Have Seen* (1918) – African American recruitment play

(The last four plays appear in *War Plays by Women: An International Anthology* edited by Claire Tylee, Elaine Turner and Agnès Cardinal, 1999)

- The film *Shoulder Arms* (Chaplin, 1918).

Fig. 1 *Actor and playwright Miles Malleson*

■ Questions

AO1: Developing an informed response to the text

- ■ What is happening in this scene?
- ■ What is your response to the different characters and their attitudes to the war?

AO2: Understanding how structure, form and language shape meaning

- ■ What do you find interesting about the ways Malleson creates the character of Harold?
- ■ How does he structure the dialogue?
- ■ Explore the ways the interaction of characters creates dramatic effects.
- ■ What use does Malleson make of stage directions?

AO3: Exploring connections, comparisons and the interpretations of other readers

- ■ Compare the presentation of Harold with that of other male characters in plays about World War One.
- ■ Compare the ways Malleson writes about the enemy with other references in your wider reading.
- ■ Does the presentation of Mr Gould and the Colonel find echoes in your wider reading?
- ■ A cabinet minister described the play as a 'deliberate calumny' on the British soldier. How do you react to this view?

AO4: Understanding the significance and influence of contexts

- ■ Explore the ways the extract from the play uses the World War One context.
- ■ What does it have to tell you about the position of women?
- ■ Why do you think the play was censored?

■ Drama in the years after the war

After the war, plays that took the war as their subject appeared only slowly, and when they did they tended not to be graphic.

Shaw's *Heartbreak House* appeared in 1921. It portrays the English upper classes on the eve of war as idle, self-obsessed and doomed. Shaw does not ever show soldiers in combat, but is far more concerned with political and social analysis.

The problem remained of how to represent the war and describe the trauma. Generally, playwrights of the 1920s and 1930s struggled to get plays about the war staged; it seemed that no theatre manager was willing to take on a play with a moral and historical purpose.

Journey's End (1929) was the first play to represent trench life realistically on the stage. It also dramatised the effects of prolonged service at the front on officers, some of whom resorted to alcohol to counteract shell shock and deaden the pain of losing their men. It depicts the claustrophobia and the terror of the invisible enemy. If you are not studying this play for Unit 2 coursework, you should certainly include it in your wider reading.

In the 1930s there were many performances of plays about horror, crime and spies, but there was little direct confrontation of the war in the theatre. Coward's *Post Mortem* was never performed. It attacked the church and state, and also condemned the public for their stupidity. Somerset Maugham's *For Services Rendered* (1932) closed after 78 performances. It focused on the Ardsleys, a broken family with a son blinded by the war. Muriel Box wrote her *Angels of War*, about female ambulance drivers, in 1935, but it was not performed until 1981. This text would clearly make an interesting companion to Helen Zenna Smith's *Not So Quiet*.

The extracts in this section come from *The Silver Tassie* by Sean O'Casey. O'Casey was an idealist with a strong sense of justice and he wrote this bleak play between 1926 and 1928. He had shown earlier interest in and concern about World War One when he wrote three plays about the slums of Dublin. The third of these plays – *The Plough and the Stars*, which dealt with the Irish citizen army and the Easter Rising – provoked a public outcry because he refused to glorify the violence of the nationalist movement. Instead, he mocked the heroics of war and showed that dead heroes were far outnumbered by dead and innocent people. He followed these plays with *The Silver Tassie*, a powerful indictment of the waste of war, which he submitted to the Abbey Theatre in 1927. It was rejected by W.B. Yeats and the Abbey managers. Yeats insisted that it was 'all anti-war propaganda to the exclusion of plot and character'.

The play focused on the price the common people have to pay for the stupidities of war, dramatising the tragedy of young men disabled in the war. O'Casey felt the need to represent the working classes in a reaction against Sherriff's *Journey's End*, which he called 'that backboneless and ribless play'. He tells the story of Harry Heegan and represents him first at the peak of his athleticism as a footballer, then as a soldier, then as a survivor, then disabled and wheelchair bound with his life destroyed.

For three of its four acts, the play is a conventional melodrama: Act 1 shows the soldier on the last day of his leave winning a football match and the silver tassie; Act 3 shows him in hospital recuperating from his injuries; and Act 4 sees him in a wheelchair at the football club watching everyone – including his ex-girlfriend – celebrating the end of the war. In Act 2, however, O'Casey created an **expressionistic** and poetic vision of the nightmare of the Front Line as it was experienced by the common soldiers. This Act, attacking both Christianity and its militancy, was set in a generic war zone. It featured a symbolic set, a two-dimensional satirised authority figure, anonymised characters, chanting and rhythmic movement.

O'Casey's anger at the human cost of the war is evident. The play was finally staged in 1935.

Extracts B1 and B2

There follow two extracts from *The Silver Tassie*. In the first we witness the return of Harry Heegan from his triumph on the football field before he returns to the war. In the second extract, he returns to the football club to 'celebrate' the end of the war.

Extract B1

Susie (*who has been looking out of the window, excitedly*) They're comin', they're comin': a crowd with a concertina; some of them carrying Harry on their shoulders, an' others are carrying that Jessie Taite too, holding a silver cup in her hands. Oh, look at the shameful way she's showing her legs to all who like to have a look at them!

Mrs Heegan Never mind Jessie's legs – what we have to do is hurry him out in time to catch the boat.

The sound of a concertina playing in the street outside has been heard, and the noise of a marching crowd. The crowd stops at the house. Shouts are heard – 'Up the Avondales!'; 'Up Harry Heegan and the Avondales!' Then steps are heard coming up the stairs, and first Simon Norton enters, holding the door ceremoniously wide open to allow Harry to enter, with his arm around Jessie, who is carrying a silver cup joyously, rather than reverentially, elevated, as a priest would elevate a chalice. Harry is wearing khaki trousers, a military cap stained with trench mud, a vivid orange-coloured jersey with black collar and cuffs. He is twenty-three years of age, tall, with the sinewy muscles of a manual worker made flexible by athletic sport. He is a typical young worker, enthusiastic, very often boisterous, sensible by instinct rather than by reason. He has gone to the trenches as unthinkingly as he would go to the polling booth. He isn't naturally stupid; it is the stupidity of persons in high places that has stupefied him. He has given all to his masters, strong heart, sound lungs, healthy stomach, lusty limbs and the little mind that education has permitted to develop sufficiently to make all the rest a little more useful. He is excited now with the sweet and innocent insanity of a fine achievement, and the rapid lowering of a few drinks.

Jessie is twenty-two or so, responsive to all the animal impulses of life. Ever dancing around, in and between the world, the flesh, and the devil. She would be happy climbing with a boy among the heather on Howth Hill, and could play ball with young men on the swards of the Phoenix Park. She gives her favour to the prominent and popular. Harry is her favourite: his strength and speed has won the Final for his club, he wears the ribbon of the DCM. It is a time of spiritual and animal exaltation for her.

Barney Bagnal, a soldier mate of Harry's, stands a little shyly near the door, with a pleasant, good-humoured grin on his rather broad face. He is the same age as Harry, just as strong, but not so quick, less finely formed, and not so sensitive; able to take most things quietly, but savage and wild when he becomes enraged. He is fully dressed, with topcoat buttoned on him, and he carries Harry's on his arm.

Harry (*joyous and excited*) Won, won, won, be-God; by the odd goal in five. Lift it up, lift it up, Jessie, sign of youth, sign of strength, sign of victory!

Mrs Heegan (*to Sylvester*) I knew, now, Harry would come back in time to catch the boat.

Harry (*to Jessie*) Leave it here, leave it down here, Jessie, under the picture, the picture of the boy that won the final.

Extract B2

The band suddenly stops playing, and the couples seen just then through the doorway stop dancing and look attentively up the hall. After a slight pause, Harry in his chair, pushed by Susie, comes in through the entrance; his face is pale and drawn, his breath comes in quick faint gasps, and his head is leaning sideways on the back of the chair. Mrs Heegan is on one side of Harry, and Surgeon Maxwell, who is in dinner-jacket style of evening dress, wearing his medals, including the DSO, walks on the other. Harry is wheeled over near the open window. Barney and Jessie, standing in the entrance, look on and listen.

Surgeon Maxwell Here near the window. (*To Mrs Heegan*) He'll be all right, Mrs Heegan, in a second; a little faint – too much excitement. When he recovers a little, I'd get him home.

Harry (*faintly but doggedly*) Napoo home, napoo. Not yet. I'm all right. I'll spend a little time longer in the belly of an hour bulgin' out with merriment. Carry on.

Surgeon Maxwell Better for you to go home, Heegan.

Further reading/ viewing

Harry When they drink to the Club from the Cup – the Silver Tassie – that I won three times, three times for them – that first was filled to wet the lips of Jessie and of me – I'll go, but not yet. I'm all right; my name is yet only a shadow on the roll of honour.

Mrs Heegan Come home, Harry; you're getting' your allowance only on the undertstandin' that you take care of yourself.

Harry Get the Cup. I'll mind it here till you're ready to send it round to drink to the Avondales – on the table here beside me. Bring the Cup; I'll mind it here on the table beside me.

Surgeon Maxwell Get the Cup for him, someone.

Simon goes to the hall and returns with the Cup, which he gives to Harry.

Harry (*holding the Cup out*) A first drink again for me, for me alone this time, for the shell that hit me bursts for ever between Jessie and me. (*To Simon*) Go on, man, fill out the wine!

Surgeon Maxwell (*to Simon*) A little – just a glass. Won't do him any harm. (*To Harry*) Then you'll have to remain perfectly quiet, Heegan.

Harry The wine – fill out the wine!

Simon (*to Harry*) Red wine or white?

Harry Red wine, red like the faint remembrance of the fires in France, red wine like the poppies that spill their petals on the breasts of the dead men. No, white wine, white like the stillness of the millions that have removed their clamours from the crowd of life. No, red wine; red like the blood that was shed for you and for many for the commission of sin! (*He drinks the wine.*) Steady, Harry, and lift up thine eyes unto the hills. (*Roughly to those around him*) What are you all gaping at?

Surgeon Maxwell Now, now, Heegan – you must try to keep quiet.

Fig. 2 *From a production of **The Silver Tassie**, the scene in Extract B1*

Questions

AO1: Developing an informed response to the text
- What is happening in these two scenes from the play?
- What do you learn about Harry and how do you respond to him in each of the scenes?

AO2: Understanding how structure, form and language shape meaning
- Explore the ways the characters' interactions create dramatic effects
- How does O'Casey make use of stage directions?
- Examine the contrasting presentations of Harry in the two extracts, with a particular focus on the language used.

AO3: Exploring connections, comparisons and the interpretations of other readers
- Compare the presentation of the 'hero' figure with other male combatant figures in your wider reading.

- What connections can you find in your wider reading with this picture of a wounded, disabled soldier? (You might want to start with Wilfred Owen's poem 'Disabled'.)
- From your reading of the extracts, how far do you agree with George Bernard Shaw that this is 'a hell of a play'?
- From your reading of these two extracts, how do you respond to Yeats's criticism that the play was 'all anti-war propaganda to the exclusion of plot and character'?

AO4: Understanding the significance and influence of contexts
- How does O'Casey use the World War One context in the play?
- What attitudes to the disabled do you find here?
- What have you discovered about the role of women as portrayed here?

World War One plays after 1945

After World War Two, as you will know from reading widely in prose and poetry, writers still concerned themselves with World War One, but this was a relatively lean period for drama about World War One, with one significant exception: *Oh! What a Lovely War* by Joan Littlewood. Before we turn to an extract from this play, we take a look at other plays written in the post-1945 period. Given that a significant amount of time has passed since the war, it will be interesting to explore changes and developments in writers' attitudes to the war.

Hamp was written by John Wilson in 1964; it is a play about the trial and execution of the shell-shocked Private Hamp. The play became the basis for Joseph Losey's film, *King and Country*. The focus is on the officially forgotten casualties of war – the deserters. No fewer than 306 such young men were executed during World War One. The 1917 Battle of Passchendaele is the setting for the play, which is structured in three scenes – the interrogation, the trial and the execution. Hamp has been fighting since 1914 and has used up his personal store of bravery by the time of his attempted desertion three years later. Wilson is concerned to show not a coward but a man simply shocked by the horror. Shell-shocked and witless, he crawls out of a hole during the battle and walks away. He is court-martialled for desertion in the face of the enemy and, as he cannot say he would not do it again, it is decreed he has to meet a death as unceremonious as the army can make it – he is shot by his own friends.

The Love of a Good Man by Howard Barker was first produced in 1978. This play is rarely performed this side of the Atlantic. It casts a cynical eye upon traditional attitudes to the war and the activities of the War Graves Commission. Its story unfolds in 1920, two years after the war, when what is left of the British and other corpses is being dug up and buried in Belgium. Barker focuses on the hypocrisy of the ruling class, the class warfare, the thrust for profit, the weakness of the monarchy, and the swift forgetting of all the soldiers who went to their death – their only reward a narrow burial plot. At the centre of the play is the rush to get the cemetery ready before a visit by the Prince of Wales. Set in a bleak landscape and peopled by a variety of eccentric and bizarre characters, the play looks at the emotional scars of war as well as the cynicism and corruption that accompany it.

Oh! What a Lovely War was produced as a stage musical in 1963 and in 1969 became a musical film. Based on *The Donkeys* by Alan Clark, the play began life at the Theatre Royal Stratford East, produced as an ensemble production by Joan Littlewood's theatre workshop. This satirical play about World War One – and all war – was a surprise hit. A politicised and popular theatre was brought into the mainstream when it moved to the West End. The play was an upbeat mixture of documentary footage, song, music hall and other comic genres. But it was also a savage denunciation of glorifying and patriotic rhetoric.

The play is traditionally performed in pierrot costumes within a custom-made big top, featuring World War One songs. Colourful characters swap hats, helmets and sides to give a vibrant and touching account of the four key years of the war. The play was a major indictment of the horror, pity and sheer waste of the war. Harsh images of the war and shocking statistics were projected onto a backdrop, providing stark contrast with the comedy of the action in front.

Extract C

In this extract, the British Commander-in-Chief, Sir Douglas Haig, is questioned about and justifies strategic military decisions.

Haig (*entering*) Germany has shot her bolt. The prospects for 1916 are excellent.

British General (*entering*) Permission to speak, sir.

Haig Of course.

Slide 40: A map of Ypres and the surrounding district, showing Kitchener's Wood, Hill 60, Passchendaele, etc

British General If we continue in this way, the line of trenches will stretch from Switzerland to the sea. Neither we nor the Germans will be able to break through. The war will end in complete stalemate.

Haig Nonsense. We need only one more big offensive to break through and win. My troops are of fine quality, and specially trained for this type of war.

British General This is not war, sir, it is slaughter.

Haig God is with us. It is for King and Empire.

British General We are sacrificing lives at the rate of five to sometimes fifty thousand a day.

Haig One battle, our superior morale, bombardment.

Junior Officer (*entering*) Sir, tell us what to do and we'll do it.

Haig We're going to walk through the enemy lines.

British General and ***Junior Officer*** go off.

Slide 40 fades into Slide 41: Tommies advancing across no man's land, in full battle pack, silhouetted against clouds.

A man's voice, offstage, sings slowly as **Haig** *speaks.*

Fig. 3 *From a production of Oh! What a Lovely War*

Song
THERE'S A LONG, LONG TRAIL
There's a long, long trail a-winding
Into the land of my dreams,
Where the nightingale is singing
And the white moon beams...

He carries on humming the tune, ending:

... Till the day when I'll be going down that long, long trail with you.

Haig (*during the song*) Complete victory ... the destruction of German militarism ... victory march on Berlin ... slow deliberate fire is being maintained on the enemy positions ... at this moment my men are advancing across no man's land in full pack, dressing from left to right; the men are forbidden under pain of court-martial to take cover in any shell hole or dugout ... their magnificent morale will cause the enemy to flee in confusion ... the attack will be driven home with the bayonet ... I feel that every step I take is guided by the divine will.

Sounds of heavy bombardment.

Newspanel *FEBRUARY ... VERDUN ... TOTAL LOSS ONE AND A HALF MILLION MEN.*

Haig (*looking through field-glasses*) This is most unsatisfactory. Where are the Sherwood Foresters. Where are the East Lancs on the right?

British General (*who has entered during above speech*) Out in no man's land.

Haig They are sluggish from too much sitting in the trenches.

British General Most of them, sir, will never rise again.

Haig We must break through.

British General Regardless of loss, sir?

Haig The loss of, say, another 300,000 men may lead to really great results.

British General Yes, sir.

Haig And will not impede our ability to continue the offensive. In any case, we have to calculate on another great offensive next year.

British General If the slackers on the Home Front see it our way, sir.

Haig Quite.

British General We are rather short of men, sir.

Haig What's left?

British General The new chappies from Ireland have just arrived.

Haig Rather wild untrained lot! Still, they'll be raring to have a crack at the Boche, and what they lack in training, they'll make up for in gallantry.

British General They've just got off the train. Most of them haven't eaten for forty-eight hours –

Haig They are moving against a weakened and demoralised enemy. Capture the German line, without further delay.

Further reading/ viewing

- Howard Barker, *The Love of a Good Man* (1978)
- Dorothy Hewett, *The Man from Mukinupin* (1979) – a musical in celebration of Western Australian identity (in *War Plays by Women: An International Anthology* edited by Claire Tylee, Elaine Turner and Agnès Cardinal (1999)
- John Wilson, *Hamp* (1964) filmed as *King and Country* (1964)
- The film *Paths of Glory* (Kubrick, 1958)
- DVD of *Oh! What a Lovely War* (1969).

◼ Questions

AO1: Developing an informed response to the text

◼ What is happening in this scene?

◼ How do you react to the characters portrayed?

AO2: Understanding how structure, form and language shape meaning

◼ How do the slides, the song and the newspanel contribute to the dramatic effect of the scene?

◼ What do you notice about the ways the dialogue is structured?

◼ Explore the different kinds of language used.

AO3: Exploring connections, comparisons and the interpretations of other readers

◼ Compare the presentation of Haig with that of other commanding officers in other plays, novels and poems.

◼ Compare the ways this scene presents loss of life with the ways it is presented in your wider reading.

◼ How far do you agree with the view that this play is a 'savage, satirical sideswipe at the management and waste of life seen in World War One'?

AO4: Understanding the significance and influence of contexts

◼ Explore the presentation of the World War One context.

◼ What evidence is there of later 20th-century attitudes to World War One?

◼ Plays after 1945 continued – World War One meets sitcom

Late 20th-century popular culture generally paid respect to the veterans of the war and acknowledged the trauma experienced. In 1989 the fourth series of the farcical, politically combative historical television sitcom, *Blackadder*, written by Richard Curtis and Ben Elton, was shown to the nation. *Blackadder Goes Forth* consisted of six 30-minute programmes set in World War One. Blackadder himself is a cynical (almost modern) voice, commenting on and deflating the pretensions and stupidity of those around him as well as the more ludicrous and insane follies of history – in this case World War One.

These six episodes are set in 1917 on the Western Front in the trenches. Another big push is planned and Captain Blackadder's one aim is to avoid getting shot; he is constantly plotting escape. Other characters of note are the idealistic Edwardian George, the servant Baldrick and General Melchett, who rallies troops from a considerable distance, assisted by Captain Darling.

The final episode is famous for its poignancy. It sees all the characters venturing forward and charging off to die in the fog and smoke of no-man's-land. There are no closing titles, the picture simply fades from the protagonists charging across no man's land under fire to a field of poppies in the sunlight. They have been sent to silence. This tragic, sudden and bitter end, coming after riotous laughter, is shocking for viewers, and shows that this episode had the capacity to be more than just an episode of a television sitcom.

Extract D

Here is the ending of the final episode.

> **George** I'm scared, sir.
>
> **Baldrick** I'm scared too, sir.
>
> **George** I'm the last of the tiddly-winking leapfroggers from the golden summer of 1914. I don't want to die … I'm not really over keen on dying at all, sir.
>
> **Blackadder** How are you feeling, Darling?

Darling Ahm – not all that good, Blackadder. Rather hoped I'd get through the whole show, go back to work at Pratt and Sons, keep wicket for the Croydon gentlemen, marry Doris. Made a note in my diary on the way here. Simply says: 'Bugger'.

Blackadder Well, quite.

Outside is heard the muffled faraway cry: 'Stand to, stand to, fix bayonets!'

Come on, come on, let's move.

They all move out. At the door, Blackadder turns to George.

Don't forget your stick, Lieutenant.

George (*Picking up his stick*) Rather, sir. Wouldn't want to face a machine-gun without this.

They emerge in the misty trenches and all stand in a line, ready for the off. Then suddenly there is silence. The machine-guns stop.

Darling I say, listen – our guns have stopped.

George You don't think …

Baldrick Perhaps the war's over. Perhaps it's peace.

George Hurrah! The big nobs have got round a table and yanked the iron out of the fire.

Darling Thank God – we lived through it – The Great War, 1914 to 1917.

All Three Hip hip hurray!!!

Blackadder I'm afraid not. The guns have stopped because we are about to attack. Not even our generals are mad enough to shell their own men. They feel it's more sporting to let the Germans do it.

George So, we are, in fact, going over. This is, as they say, it?

Blackadder Yes, unless I can think of something very quickly.

A command is heard: 'Company, one pace forward.' They all take one step forward.

Baldrick There's a nasty splinter on that ladder, sir. A bloke could hurt himself on that.

A call: 'Stand ready.' They put their hands on the ladders, ready to climb over.

I have a plan, sir.

Blackadder Really, Baldrick, a cunning and subtle one?

Baldrick Yes, sir.

Blackadder As cunning as a fox who's just been appointed Professor of Cunning at Oxford University?

Baldrick Yes, sir.

Another call is heard: 'On the signal, Company will advance.'

Blackadder Well, I'm afraid it's too late. Whatever it was, I'm sure it was better than my plan to get out of this by pretending to be mad. I mean, who would have noticed another madman round here?

A whistle goes. He looks at Baldrick.

Good luck, everyone.

Blackadder blows his whistle. There is a roar of voices – everyone leaps up the ladders. As they rise above the sandbags they are met by thunderous machine-gunfire.

Blackadder, Baldrick, George and Darling run on, brandishing their hand-guns. They will not get far.

Silence falls. Our soldiers fade away. No Man's Land turns slowly into a peaceful field of poppies. The only sound is that of a bird, singing sweetly.

■ **Further reading**

■ Script of *Blackadder Goes Forth*, published by Penguin.

Fig. 4 *From Blackadder Goes Forth*

■ Questions

AO1: Developing an informed response to the text

■ What is happening in this scene?

■ How do you respond to the events and to the characters?

AO2: Understanding how structure, form and language shape meaning

■ Explore the ways the dialogue is structured.

■ What dramatic effects are created by the interactions of the characters and by the language they use?

■ Examine the ways the comic and the tragic are intermingled, and the dramatic effects.

■ What use is made of stage directions?

AO3: Exploring connections, comparisons and the interpretations of other readers

■ Compare this realisation of trench life with its portrayal in your wider reading.

■ Compare the attitudes to battle and to war expressed here with those presented in your wider reading.

■ Compare the attitudes presented here to commanding officers and their decisions with those you have met in your wide reading.

■ How do you respond to the view that *Blackadder* is 'no more than a politically combative sitcom'?

AO4: Understanding the significance and influence of contexts

■ Explore the ways the World War One context is used here.

■ What evidence do you find of later 20th-century attitudes to the war?

■ World War One drama from the 1980s to the present day

Two plays written and first performed in the 1980s are in the set text list for Unit 1 coursework. These are *The Accrington Pals* (1981), which explores the effects of government propaganda and recruiting strategies on a community, and *Not about Heroes* (1982), which traces the meeting and friendship of Wilfred Owen and Siegfried Sassoon. If you have not chosen to study either of these texts then they should form an integral part of your wider reading.

Nick Whitby's *To the Green Fields Beyond* was first performed in 2000. It features a multiracial crew of a tank during the Somme offensive in 1916. There was great hope that this weapon would provide a major breakthrough and the tank corps was drawn from all corners of the Empire. The cast includes a West Indian and an Irish man, reminding the audience of the contribution and sacrifices from the Commonwealth.

In 2005 Tom Stoppard's translation of Gerald Sibleyras's *Le Vent des Peupliers*, taking the English title *Heroes*, was performed. It focuses on forgotten veterans in a French old people's home in 1959. It plays up their eccentricities and foibles and is a gentle observation of old age, memory and future hope. Tom Stoppard talks of the play as 'characters in exquisite pain'.

The extracts we are going to consider in this section are taken from *Observe the Sons of Ulster Marching Towards the Somme* by Frank McGuinness (1989). His focus is on the ordinary soldiers who responded to Kitchener's call for volunteers as the Regular Army and Territorial resources were exhausted. He explores the complex situation of men from different traditions in Northern Ireland who fought side by side on the Somme. The writer is a Catholic from Donegal, but his play focuses on eight Protestant Ulstermen (the 36th Ulster division) as they fight – and nearly all die – in the World War One Battle of the Somme. The Somme Battle on the first of July is the anniversary of the Battle of the Boyne in 1690. The two battles have a special and sacred place for Loyalist Protestants, marking the Union sealed with blood. McGuinness portrays the men sensitively and sympathetically, both as individuals and representatives of a culture, but does not flinch from showing the militant bigotry of their culture's political and religious aspects. The play has become a beacon for cross-cultural understanding and the response in reviews is invariably positive.

The play deliberately undermines stereotypical understandings of sect, violence and sex. It is also a play of memory, so it explores the ways past and present shape each other.

Pyper is the one character who survives the Somme and acts as a catalyst through the play, forcing each of the soldiers to consider what it means to be an Ulsterman, a Protestant and a subject of the Empire.

Extracts E1 and E2

We look here at two extracts from the play, one from near the beginning, and one from the end.

In the first extract, Pyper is an old man and he frames the action with a deathbed soliloquy speech recalling, from the vantage point of old age in 1969, the loss of his comrades half a century before. After the speech, the play switches to the events of 1916 and the young Pyper takes the stage.

In the second extract, as the men move into battle, their individual conflicts are forgotten and they have affirmed a communal identity.

Extract E1

Pyper I will not apologise for that outburst before you. You know I am given to sudden fits like that. The shock you gave never left my system entirely. I still see you ghosts. Very infrequently. During daylight now. Dear Lord, you are kind in your smaller mercies. Did you intend that we should keep seeing ghosts? It was the first sign that your horrors had shaken us into madness. Some were lucky enough to suffer your visions immediately. Those I belonged to, those I have not forgotten, the irreplaceable ones, they kept their nerve, and they died. I survived. No, survival was not my lot. Darkness, for eternity, is not survival.

(Silence.)

There is a type of man who invites death upon himself. I thought once this is the stuff heroes are made from. I enlisted in the hope of death. I would be such a man. But mine was not the stuff of heroes. Those with me were heroes because they died without complaint for what they believed in. They taught me, by the very depth of their belief, to believe. To believe in you. What sense could you make of their sacrifice? I at least continued their work in this province. The freedom of faith they fought and died for would be maintained. There would be, and there will be no surrender. The sons of Ulster will rise and lay their enemy low, as they did at the Boyne, as they did at the Somme, against any invader who will trespass on to their homeland. Fenians claim a Cuchullian as their ancestor, but he is ours, for they lay down for centuries and wept in their sorrow, but we took up arms and fought against an ocean. An ocean of blood. His blood is our inheritance. Not theirs. Sinn Fein? Ourselves alone. It is we, the Protestant people, who have always stood alone. We have stood alone and triumphed, for we are God's chosen.

(Silence.)

Leave me. Do not possess me. I do not wish to be your chosen.

(Silence.)

I'm a fool. A liar. I've learned nothing from you but how to preach in your name. You have never forgiven that I started out wrong. I looked on my family, my traditions, my faith, with greatest cynicism. It is your curse upon me. I have to learn the hard way. After the war, for you, I had to be different again. To be extreme. The world lay in ruins about my feet. I wanted to rebuild it in the image of my fallen companions. I owed them that much. I came back to this country and managed my father's estates. I helped organise the workings of this province. A small role. Nothing of import. Was that also what you decreed? Leave me. Must I remember? Yes, I remember. I remember the sky was pink, extraordinarily pink. There were men from Coleraine, talking about salmon fishing. A good man who wanted to enter the Church gave me an orange sash. We sang hymns and played football. That is true, football. Someone said the sky is red today. David said it's pink. And I looked and I could see again. I saw the sky in him. I knew he would die, for he was turning from earth into air.

(Silence. As the light increases, PYPER sees the ghosts appear, CRAIG, ROULSTON and CRAWFORD)

Extract E2

Moore: I can see the others gathering.

Millen: It's time then.

Mcilwaine: All together.

Crawford: Better move.

Roulston: Every one.

Craig: Right.

Anderson: Last stage.

(With the exception of PYPER, they each begin to put on their Orange sashes. CRAIG watches PYPER, then takes his sash off, goes to MOORE, hands it to him. MOORE hesitates, then exchanges his sash for CRAIG'S. At this there is an exchange of sashes, CRAWFORD'S for ANDERSON'S, MILLEN'S for MCILWAINE'S. ROULSTON goes to PYPER, who takes ROULSTON'S and gives him his own.)

Pyper: It's come to this, Roulston?

Roulston: What's decreed passes, Pyper.

Pyper: There's no fight back?

Roulston: There's just the fight.

Pyper: The good fight?

Roulston: The everlasting fight.

Pyper: Inside us?

Roulston: And outside us.

Pyper: Preach.

Roulston: No. You preach.

(Silence. They wait.)

You believe. Believe.

(Silence.)

Fig. 5 *From a production of **Observe the Sons of Ulster Marching Towards the Somme***

Pyper: God in heaven, if you hear the words of man, I speak to you this day. I do it now to ask we be spared. I do it to ask for strength. Strength for these men around me, strength for myself. If you are a just and merciful God, show your mercy this day. Save us. Save our country. Destroy our enemies at home and on this field of battle. Let this day at the Somme be as glorious in the memory of Ulster as that day at the Boyne, when you scattered our enemies. Lead us back from this exile. To Derry, to the Foyle. To Belfast and the Lagan. To Armagh. To Tyrone. To the Bann and its banks. To Erne and its islands. Protect them. Protect us. Protect me. Let us fight bravely. Let us win gloriously. Lord, look down on us. Spare us. I love – . Observe the sons of Ulster marching towards the Somme. I love their lives. I love my own life. I love my home. I love my Ulster. Ulster. Ulster. Ulster. Ulster. Ulster. Ulster. Ulster. Ulster.

(As the chant of 'Ulster' commences rifles and bayonets are raised. The chant turns into a battle cry, reaching frenzy. The ELDER PYPER appears. His YOUNGER SELF sees him. The chant ceases.)

Younger Pyper: Ulster.

Elder Pyper: Ulster.

Younger Pyper: I have seen horror.

Further reading

- Alan Bleasdale, *The Monocled Mutineer* (1986) – a BBC-TV script adapted from the book by William Allison and John Fairley
- Stephen Macdonald, *Not About Heroes* (first performed 1982)
- Tom Stoppard's translation of Gerald Sibleyras's *Heroes* (*Le Vent des Peupliers*)
- Peter Whelan, *The Accrington Pals* (first performed 1981)
- Nick Whitby, *To the Green Fields Beyond* (first performed 2000)
- Wendy Lill, *The Fighting Days* (1984) – episodes in the life of a Canadian suffragist
- Christina Reid, *My Name, Shall I Tell You My Name* (1988) – focus on World War One and the troubles in Northern Ireland

(The last two plays are to be found in *War Plays by Women: An International Anthology* edited by Claire Tylee, Elaine Turner and Agnès Cardinal, 1999).

Elder Pyper: Ulster.

Younger Pyper: They kept their nerve, and they died.

Elder Pyper: Ulster.

Younger Pyper: There would be, and there will be, no surrender.

Elder Pyper: Ulster.

Younger Pyper: The house has grown cold, the province has grown lonely.

Elder Pyper: Ulster.

Younger Pyper: You'll always guard Ulster.

Elder Pyper: Ulster.

Younger Pyper: Save it.

Elder Pyper: Ulster.

Younger Pyper: The temple of the Lord is ransacked.

Elder Pyper: Ulster.

(PYPER reaches towards himself.)

Younger Pyper: Dance in this deserted temple of the Lord.

Elder Pyper : Dance.

(Darkness.)

Questions

AO1: Developing an informed response to the text
- What happens in the two scenes?
- What are your thoughts and feelings about the characters presented?

AO2: Understanding how structure, form and language shape meaning
- What is interesting about the ways the writer presents the characters?
- What dramatic effects does he create from their interactions?
- Explore the ways the dialogue is structured.
- What use is made of stage directions?
- What dramatic use is made of the Elder Pyper?

AO3: Exploring connections, comparisons, and the interpretations of other readers
- Compare the presentation of Pyper in each extract, noting how ideas have been developed.
- Compare Pyper with other portrayals of World War One soldiers encountered in your wider reading.
- Compare this portrayal of Irish experience with other writings by Irish writers – you could start with the novel *A Long Long Way*, or perhaps *The Silver Tassie*.
- How do you respond to the view that as 'a memory play, it examines the ways in which past and present shape each other'?

AO4: Understanding the significance and influence of contexts
- What use does McGuiness make of the World War One context?
- What picture of Irishness do we see here?

Summary

- In this chapter you have studied extracts from five different plays written about World War One. These extracts, and the background information, should give you a good overview of the style and subject matter of World War One drama. You will be able to use these ideas when answering the context question in the AS examination. We will be looking at the context question in more detail, and how to approach it, in the next chapter.

7   Tackling the context question

Aims of the chapter:

- Introduce the context question in the Unit 1 examination.

- Shows how the relevant Assessment Objectives are expressed in the key words of the question.

- Makes meaning from studying the context extract, identifying key features of content and style.

- Makes connections between the context question extract and wider reading in the area of study.

The **context question** in Unit 1 is at the heart of the AS English Literature course. It is the question where you have the opportunity to demonstrate and use the knowledge you have gained from all the reading you have done throughout the course.

Preparation

In previous chapters, we have already looked at how you will approach:

- the set text poetry question
- the coursework prose task
- the coursework prose and drama comparison
- the wider reading prose texts
- the wider reading drama texts
- the wider reading poetry texts.

The examination question

The non-fiction text

All the reading and the exercises you have done in your course are relevant to the **context question**, which will be based on an extract from a **non-fiction** text. This may be any of the following:

- a diary
- a letter
- an autobiography
- a biography
- literary criticism
- a history text
- cultural commentary.

The question will include the extract, which you will need to read and study carefully. The examiner will give you information about how and when the extract came to be written. The question will then ask you to:

- consider the writer's **thoughts and feelings** about the war and the ways in which he (or she) expresses them

- compare the extract with your wider reading, saying **how typical** you think it is of writing about World War One literature. You should consider both subject matter and **style**.

The Assessment Objectives and the link to key words in the examination question

You can see how all four Assessment Objectives are assessed in this question:

AO1: Communicating your informed, coherent response to the text – is always tested in all questions.

AO2: Understanding and analysing how writers' choices of form, structure and language shape meaning – is tested in the first bullet point with the words 'the ways he (or she) expresses them' and in the second bullet point in the word style.

AO3: Exploring connections and comparisons as well as the interpretations of other readers – is tested in the first bullet point where you are asked to consider what the writer's thoughts and feelings might be, and in the second bullet point where the examiner asks you to compare the extract with your wider reading.

AO4: Using your understanding of the significance and influence of contexts – is tested in the second bullet point where the examiner asks how typical this extract is of writing about World War One.

Practising the skills

We are now going to look at **five** extracts so that you can see how to:

■ read the extract carefully

■ look for evidence of the writer's thoughts and feelings (**AO1**)

■ analyse the writer's choices of form, structure and language and how they shape meaning (**AO2**)

■ make connections between the extract and your wider reading (**AO3**)

■ assess the typicality of attitude and style of the extract (**AO4**).

Extract A

Read the following information about the writer and the book from which the extract is taken. Then read the extract carefully.

Bernard Bergonzi's study of the literature of World War One, *Heroes' Twilight*, was published in 1965. In the Preface he says he is 'concerned, principally, with literary analysis and assessment'. The following short extract is taken from the first chapter where he is reflecting on the literature of war through the ages.

> The war of 1914–1918 can still very properly be referred to by its original name of the Great War; for despite the greater magnitude of its more truly global successor, it represented a far more radical crisis in British civilisation. In particular, it meant that the traditional mythology of heroism and the hero, the Hotspurian mode of self-assertion, had ceased to be viable; even though heroic deeds could be, and were, performed in abundance.

> ■ **Did you know?**
>
> Hotspur was a character in Shakespeare's play *Henry IV Part One*. Above all else he passionately craved the 'honour' that came from success in battle.

■ **Further reading**

Literary and cultural criticism and biography:

■ Adrian Barlow, *The Great War in British Literature* (2000)

■ Paul Fussell, *The Great War and Modern Memory* (1975)

■ Robert Giddings, *The War Poets, The Lives and Writings of the 1914–1918 War Poets* (1988)

■ Dominic Hibberd, *Wilfred Owen, A New Biography* (2002)

■ Samuel Hynes, *A War Imagined: The First World War and English Culture* (1992)

■ *A Companion to Modern British and Irish Drama 1880–2005*, ed. Mary Luckhurst pp301–16 (2006)

■ Jon Silkin, *Out of Battle: The Poetry of the Great War* (1972)

■ Jon Stallworthy, *Wilfred Owen* (1974)

■ D.S.R. Welland, *Wilfred Owen, A Critical Study* (1960)

■ Jay Winter, *Sites of Memory, Sites of Mourning* (1995)

🔍 Questions for you to consider

- What key point is Bergonzi making about the literature of World War One? (AO1)
- What do you notice about the ways he expresses this key point? (AO2)
- What kind of vocabulary does he use and what references does he make? (AO2)
- What influence do you think the time of writing might have on his viewpoint? (AO4)
- What connections can you make between Bergonzi's view of the literature of World War One as he expresses it here and views expressed in your wider reading? (You might like to start with those texts that address the notions of 'hero/heroes'.) (AO3)
- Which texts support his view? Try to think of at least **one** prose, **one** drama and **one** poetry text/extract. (AOs 3 and 4)
- Which texts challenge the key point he makes here? Try to think of at least **one** prose, **one** drama and **one** poetry text/extract. (AOs 3 and 4)
- Assess the **typicality** of the extract. (AO4)
- If you are working in a group, share and compare your findings.

Extract B

Read the following information about the writer and the book from which the extract is taken. Then read the extract carefully.

For his book *Last Post* (published in 2005), Max Arthur found and interviewed the last 21 British veterans of World War One. The writer allows the men to describe their experiences in their own words, recording their oral testimony. In this extract, Cecil Withers (1898–2005) of the 17th Battalion Royal Fusiliers describes conditions on the Somme.

> It's important that people know what it was like. I remember once, on the Somme, seeing half a dozen of our English boys, all in pieces in a big shell hole. They were half buried, stinking. It was hot and there was a terrible stench and they were covered in bluebottles and cockroaches. It was a terrible sight. Those poor boys. It made me sick. We had to smoke strong Turkish cigarettes to hide the smell. On the firestep in the trenches during the night, you could hear the groaning of the dying – but you couldn't go out to help them. There were rats feeding on their flesh. They were lying there, dying in pain and misery, and the rats were nibbling away at their flesh. Cockroaches did that as well, they fed on their blood.
>
> People still talk a lot of rubbish about the war. I've always let people know what really went on. I suppose I was breaking the rules. I've let people know so that the truth could be a warning to them. When the war was going on, its horrors were kept quiet and the full display of dreadful things only came out afterwards. These things were carefully hidden at the time.

■ Further reading

Oral testimony and historical research on World War One:

- *Forgotten Voices of The Great War*, ed. Max Arthur (2002)
- Richard Holmes, *Tommy* (2005)
- Lyn Macdonald, *Somme* (1983)
- Lyn Macdonald, *The Roses of No Man's Land* (1993)
- Ben McIntyre, *A Foreign Field* (2001)
- Richard Van Emden, *The Trench* (2002)

Questions for you to consider

- What are the thoughts and feelings about the war expressed by Cecil Withers in this extract? (AO1)
- What do you notice about the ways in which he expresses himself? (AO2)
- What influence do you think the time of composition and the gender of the writer might have on the writing? (AO4)
- What connections can you make between Withers' descriptions of and views about the war and those expressed in your wider reading? (For example, what pictures of the battlefield are there in your wider reading? And which texts can you think of that examine the gap between the Home Front and the Western Front?) (AO3)
- Which texts support his views? Try to think of at least **one** prose, **one** drama and **one** poetry text/extract. (AOs 3 and 4)
- Which texts challenge his views? Try to think of at least **one** prose, **one** drama and **one** poetry text/extract. (AOs 3 and 4)
- Assess the **typicality** of the extract. (AO4)
- If you are working in a group, share and compare your findings.

Q **Fig. 1** *Battle of the Somme*

Extract C

Read the following information about the writer and the book from which the extract is taken. Then read the extract carefully.

This extract is taken from Vera Brittain's autobiography, *Testament of Youth* (published 1933). It describes the aftermath of the death of her fiancé, Roland Leighton, who was killed in the trenches in December 1915.

In Sussex, by the end of January, the season was already on its upward grade; catkins hung bronze from the bare, black branches, and in the damp lanes between Hassocks and Keymer the birds sang loudly. How I hated them as I walked back to the station one late afternoon, when a red sunset turned the puddles on the road into gleaming pools of blood, and a new horror of mud and death darkened my mind with its dreadful obsession. Roland, I reflected bitterly, was now part of the corrupt clay into which the war had transformed the fertile soil of France; he would never again know the smell of a wet evening in the early spring.

I had arrived at the cottage that morning to find his mother and sister standing in helpless distress in the midst of his returned kit, which was lying, just opened, all over the floor. The garments sent back included the outfit that he had been wearing when he was hit. I wondered, and I wonder still, why it was thought necessary to return such relics – the tunic torn back and front by the bullet, a khaki vest dark and stiff with blood, and a pair of blood-stained breeches slit open at the top by someone obviously in a violent hurry. Those gruesome rags made me realise, as I had never realised before, all that France really meant. Eighteen months afterwards the smell of Etaples village, though fainter and more diffused, brought back to me the memory of those poor remnants of patriotism.

Fig. 2 *A soldier's kit and uniform*

Questions for you to consider

- What are Brittain's thoughts and feelings about the war as expressed in this extract? (AO1)

- What do you notice about the ways in which she expresses these thoughts and feelings? Look first at the vocabulary she chooses and how it shapes meaning, then look at how she structures her thoughts and consider how effective this structuring is in communicating her thoughts and feelings. (AO2)

- What influence do you think the time of composition and the gender of the writer might have had on the text? (AO4)

- What connections can you make between Brittain's thoughts and feelings and those you have discovered in your wider reading? (AOs 3 and 4)

- How does this autobiographical extract compare with other autobiographies from World War One that you have read? You should consider both subject matter and style. (AOs 3 and 4)

- Which other texts from your wider reading support Brittain's views about the war? Try to think of at least **one** prose, **one** drama and **one** poetry text/extract. (AOs 3 and 4)

- Which texts from your wider reading challenge Brittain's views about the war? Try to think of at least **one** prose, **one** drama and **one** poetry text/extract. (AOs 3 and 4)

- Assess the **typicality** of the extract. (AO4)

- If you are working as a group, share and compare your findings.

Further reading

World War One memoirs:

- Richard Aldington, *Life for Life's Sake* (1941)

- Edmund Blunden, *Undertones of War* (1928)

- Robert Graves, *Good-bye to All That* (1929)

- Siegfried Sassoon, *Siegfried's Journey* (1945)

Extract D

Read the following information about the writer and the book from which the extract is taken. Then read the extract carefully.

A War in Words, edited by Svetlana Palmer and Sarah Wallis and published in 2003, tells the story of World War One through the diaries and letters of its combatants, eyewitnesses and victims. This extract is taken from the diary of Robert Cude, who was on messenger duty when the bombardment of the Somme began at 7.22am on 1 July 1916, a warm and sunny day.

1st July
The day of the attack arrives and the guns are really deafening, never a German can live over that side. As the time wears on and gets nearer to the appointed hour I am wondering how many such bombardments will be necessary before war is finished. This must be the beginning of the end.

7.22a.m. Every gun for eight minutes gave of their best and the din was terrific.

Punctual to time 7.28 a.m. two minutes before the line advanced Captain Neville, 8th E. Surreys, kicks off the football that is to take the boys across to Jerry. He is killed as his leg is uplifted after kicking the ball. I am too busy to take in the surroundings other than our immediate front. E. Surreys and Queens go over singing and shouting and the ball is punted from one to another. They are followed by the 7th Buffs who are mopping up, their time will come if Jerry is refractory. Soon after the lads get going; we can see that, contrary to expectations, we are not to have things all our own way. Here I may add that I am up forward on a message and determined to stop and see a bit of the fun. Jerry's machine gun opens a terrific fire on our chaps and the first wave is speedily decimated. Others jump forward and fill the gaps. I am aghast at the accuracy of the fire. He has plenty of machine guns, and is making a frightful carnage. I long to be with battalion so that I can do my best to bereave a German family. I hate these swines.

It is a wonderful sight and one I shall not forget. War such as this, on such a beautiful day seems to me to be quite correct and proper! On such a day as this one, one feels a keen joy in living even though living is, to say the least of it, very precarious. Men are racing to certain death, and jesting and smiling and cursing, yet wonderfully quiet in a sense for one feels that one must kill, as often as one can.

Fig. 3 *Imagine the trauma of advancing towards machine guns like this one*

Questions for you to consider

■ What are the thoughts and feelings about the war expressed by Robert Cude in this extract? (AO1)

■ What have you noticed about the ways in which he expresses himself? (AO2)

■ What influences do you think the time of writing and the gender of the writer might have on the writing? (AO4)

■ What similarities and what differences do you see between this extract and Extract B, both accounts of the war on the Somme? Consider both subject matter and style. (AOs 2 and 3)

■ What connections can you make between Cude's descriptions of and views about the war and those expressed in your wider reading? (AOs 3 and 4)

■ Which wider reading texts support his views? Try to think of at least **one** prose, **one** drama and **one** poetry text/extract. (AOs 3 and 4)

■ Which texts challenge his views? Try to think of at least **one** prose, **one** drama and **one** poetry text/extract. (AOs 3 and 4)

■ Assess the **typicality** of the extract. (AO4)

■ If you are working as a group, share and compare your findings.

Further reading

Letters and diaries:

■ *Chronicle of Youth, Vera Brittain's War Diary,* ed. Alan Bishop (1981)

■ *Letters from a Lost Generation,* ed. Alan Bishop and Mark Bostridge (1998)

■ *Women's Writing on the First World War,* ed. Agnès Cardinal, Dorothy Goldman and Judith Hattaway (1999)

■ *A Month at the Front,* Diary of an Unknown Soldier (2006)

■ Michael Walsh, *Brothers in War* (2006)

Extract E

Read the following information about the writer and the book from which the extract is taken. Then read the extract carefully.

Paul Nash was an official war artist during World War One. This extract is from a letter he wrote on 18 November 1917.

I have just returned, last night, from a visit to Brigade Headquarters up the line, and I shall not forget it as long as I live. I have seen the most frightful nightmare of a country more conceived by Dante or Poe than by nature, unspeakable, utterly undescribable. In the fifteen drawings I have made I may give you some vague idea of its horror, but only being in it and of it can ever make you sensible of its dreadful nature and of what our men in France have to face. We all have a vague notion of the terrors of a battle, and can conjure up with the aid of some of the more inspired war correspondents and the pictures in the Daily Mirror some vision of a battlefield; but no pen or drawing can convey this country – the normal setting of the battles taking place day and night, month after month. Evil and the incarnate fiend alone can be master of this war, and no glimmer of God's hand is seen anywhere. Sunset and sunrise are blasphemous, they are mockeries to man, only the black rain of the bruised and swollen clouds all through the bitter black of night is fit atmosphere in such a land. The rain drives on, the stinking mud becomes more evilly yellow, the shell holes fill up with green-white water, the roads and tracks are covered in inches of slime, the black dying trees ooze and sweat and the shells never cease. They alone plunge overhead, tearing away the rotting tree stumps, breaking the plank roads, striking down horses and mules, annihilating, maiming, maddening, they plunge into the grave which is this land; one huge grave, and cast upon it the poor dead. It is unspeakable, godless, hopeless. I am no longer an artist interested and curious, I am a messenger who will bring back the word from the men who are fighting to those who want the war to go on forever. Feeble, inarticulate will be my message, but it will have a bitter truth, and may it burn their lousy souls.

Fig. 4 *Paul Nash*

■ **Questions for you to consider**

■ What thoughts and feelings about the war are expressed by Paul Nash in this extract? (AO1)

■ Consider the ways he expresses himself and the effectiveness of the writer's choices of form, structure and language in shaping meaning. (AO2)

■ What influence do you think the time of composition, the gender of the writer and the writer's occupation might have on the writing? (AO4)

■ What connections can you make between Extracts B, D and E? Consider both subject matter and style. (AOs 2 and 3)

■ What connections can you make between Extract E and your wider reading? (AOs 3 and 4)

■ Which texts support his views? Try to think of at least **one** prose, **one** drama and **one** poetry text/extract. (AOs 3 and 4)

■ Which texts challenge his views? Try to think of at least **one** prose, **one** drama and **one** poetry text/extract. (AOs 3 and 4)

■ Assess the **typicality** of the extract. (AO4)

■ If you are working as a group, share and compare your findings.

💡 ℹ️ 🔍 *Summary*

The extracts

■ In this chapter we have looked closely at five extracts, which have ranged from literary analysis, to oral testimony, to autobiography, to diary, to memoir. The questions and activities have been devised to encourage you to look at the extracts closely and in ways that will help you in the examination.

Variety of response

■ If you have shared your thoughts with other students, you will no doubt have discovered perspectives other than your own and you will have realised that there are many different ways in which wider reading can be used. Examiners expect to come across many different ways of approaching the question and to read a variety of answers. There is no 'right' answer; but they expect you to write relevantly, addressing the key words, and to select appropriate supporting material.

The question

■ Remember that in the actual examination the question will contain two simple bullet points. In order to answer the question, however, you will need to go through all the processes that have followed each of the extracts in this chapter.

Here, to end the chapter, is an example of the context question as it will appear in the examination:

Read the following extract carefully. It is taken from the Prologue of *Life for Life's Sake*, a memoir written by Richard Aldington (1892–1962) in 1941. Aldington was a literary scholar, novelist and poet. He enlisted in 1916 and fought in France.

It is only after a war that the experience of the individual survivor seems to have either interest or value. During a war civilians can think only in terms of 'our side' and 'their side'. All they ask of their men is that they shall win. The individual suffering and cost are veiled behind military phrases, which cushion the abrupt shocks of reality. How much human misery and unrepeatable calamity lie hidden behind such words and phrases as 'curtain fire', 'local bombardment', 'clashes of patrols', 'strategic retreat', 'heavy fighting', 'advance held up', 'aerial bombing', 'casualties'! We cease to think of Jack, Jean, and Johann, and talk of Divisions and Corps. We even rejoice – it is horrible – at 'enemy casualties'. Delicate women look pleased when they hear that 'the ground in front of our positions is heaped with enemy dead'. And yet they are shocked by the simple-minded and practical cannibal who makes a meal of his enemy or his grandmother. We should not say, 'as savage as a wild beast', but 'as savage as civilised man'. How can we look on ourselves and our species with anything but disgust?

In your answer you should:

- consider the writer's thoughts and feelings about the war and the ways in which he expresses them
- compare this extract with your wider reading, saying how typical you think it is of writing of and about World War One. You should consider both subject matter and style.

Conclusion: a specimen paper

Aims of the chapter:

- Reviews the skills and knowledge gained through your AS English Literature course and using this book.

- Introduces a specimen examination paper where you can practise your skills and identify where you might need to improve them.

- Looks at ways of approaching the examination paper.

- Helps you to understand how you will be assessed.

Link

In Chapter 2 we explored the kinds of question that will be asked on your set poetry text; one of the suggested activities was to make up your own questions that addressed the three relevant Assessment Objectives.

In Chapter 7 we looked in detail at the kinds of extracts you could expect to find in the context question on the examination paper, ending the chapter with an example of a specimen context question.

Introduction

By the time you have worked through this book and are approaching your AS English Literature examination, you will need to start thinking about how you are going to:

- **use the knowledge** you have gathered, through your study of the set texts and your wider reading of literature on World War One literature, in the examination

- **demonstrate the skills** you have been practising through the **activities**.

Your coursework essays should now be written, but remember that your knowledge of your two chosen coursework texts – the play and the novel – is relevant to the context question on the examination paper. In addition, you should have a Reading Log of all the wider reading you have done in prose, poetry and drama of World War One; this log will either be in the form of written notes or a file on the computer. These notes should form the basis of your revision for the examination paper.

The specimen paper

The best way to prepare for the real examination is to practise answering questions of the type that you will be asked. You can, of course, make up your own questions – alone, or in a group, and with the help of your teacher. If you do this, you need to follow the models provided in this book.

What follows now is a complete specimen paper. How you use it will be for you to decide. You and your teacher may wish to use it as a 'mock' examination, sitting down and writing for two hours under examination conditions. Or you may wish to look at the questions alone or in a group, brainstorming what materials you might use, how you might structure your answers and then comparing notes, before you write the relevant essays.

Here is the paper. Read through it carefully and closely.

AQA Examination-style questions

Unit 1 Texts in context

Time allowed 2 hours

Candidates must answer two questions:

- the compulsory question in Section A
- one question in Section B.

OPTION B: WORLD WAR ONE LITERATURE
SECTION A: CONTEXTUAL LINKING

Answer Question 1.

1   Read the following extract carefully. It is taken from *Letters from a Lost Generation* (First World War Letters of Vera Brittain and four friends). In this letter, Vera is writing to her mother from France.

In your answer you should:

- consider the writer's thoughts and feelings about the war and the ways in which she expresses them
- compare this extract to your wider reading, saying how typical you think it is of the literature of World War One. You should consider both subject matter and style.

(45 marks)

"Vera to Edith Brittain
24th General, France, 5 December 1917

The hospital is very heavy now – as heavy as when I came; the fighting is continuing very long this year, & the convoys keep coming down, two or three a night … Sometimes in the middle of the night we have to turn people out of beds & make them sleep on the floor to make room for the more seriously ill ones that have come down from the line. We have heaps of gassed cases at present who came in a day or two ago; there are 10 in this ward alone. I wish those people who write so glibly about this being a holy war & the orators who talk so much about going on no matter how long the War lasts & what it may mean, could see a case – to say nothing of 10 cases – of mustard gas in its early stages – could see the poor things burnt and blistered all over with great mustard coloured suppurating blisters, with blinded eyes – sometimes temporally, sometimes permanently – all sticky and stuck together, & always fighting for breath, with voices a mere whisper, saying that their throats are closing & they know they will choke. The only thing one can say is that such severe cases don't last long; either they die soon or else improve – usually the former; they certainly don't reach England in the state we have them here, & yet people persist in saying that God made War, when there are such inventions of the Devil about."

OPTION A: VICTORIAN LITERATURE
SECTION B: POETRY

Up the Line to Death: ed. Brian Gardner

Answer one question from this section.

2   "An anthology which has one mood and a single focus."

How far do you agree with this assessment? In your answer you should either refer to 2 or 3 poems in detail or range more widely through the whole anthology.

(45 marks)

Or

3   Brian Gardner, the editor of this anthology, has placed the poem "High Wood" by Philip Johnstone in the Epilogue.

How far do you agree that, in terms of subject matter and style, this poem forms an appropriate conclusion to the poems in the anthology?

(45 marks)

Or

Scars Upon My Heart: ed. Catherine Reilly

4   "The poems in this collection do not deal with the realities of the war."

How far do you agree with this assessment?

In your answer, you should either refer to 2 or 3 poems in detail or range more widely through the whole collection.

(45 marks)

Or

5   Remind yourself of Vera Brittain's poem "Perhaps".

To what extent do you agree with the view that, in terms of subject matter and style, this poem is the key to the whole collection?

(45 marks)

Or

War Poetry: ed. Jon Stallworthy pp. 162–225

6   How far do you agree with the view that there is little variety in subject matter and style in the poems in this selection?

In your answer you should either refer to 2 or 3 poems in detail or range more widely through the whole selection.

(45 marks)

Or

7   Remind yourself of the poem "MCMX1V" by Philip Larkin.

To what extent do you agree that, in terms of subject matter and style, this poem is the key to the whole selection?

(45 marks)

Approaching the paper

Before you start to think about the two questions you will answer, you need to consider your approach to the examination paper. This vital preparation should include:

■ familiarity with the **Assessment Objectives** and the **marking grid**

■ **revision** of all the texts you have read during the course – this will include your two coursework texts

■ experimenting with and trying out different ways of **brainstorming and planning** your essays

■ thinking about the **use of time** in the examination – a good guide is to divide the time equally between the questions, and to spend roughly 15 minutes planning and organising each answer and 45 minutes writing it

■ being aware that **you** are the **maker of meaning** when answering these questions. The key aspect of the marking grid that you need to understand is that there is no '**prescribed content**'. All the questions invite **you** to **select** and **organise** the material that you wish to use in your answer. The examiner's task is to judge how well your choices of material and your analysis of your texts enable you to construct an argument in response to the specific question set. Obviously, your answer needs to be **relevant** and **well written**, so we will spend some time now looking at all the questions on the paper, finding the **focus** and identifying the **key words**.

> ■ Link
>
> The Assessment Objectives and marking grid are explained in Chapter 1.

> ■ Activities
>
> First of all, try to identify the focus and key words of each question. You may find it useful to do the following activities. Then you can check what you have identified with the suggested answers below.
>
> **1 Key words**
>
> Study each of the seven questions and either write down or highlight or underline what you consider to be the key words of the questions. The key words need to inform all your planning (and then your writing) since they are the way the Assessment Objectives are signalled in the question.
>
> **2 The focus**
>
> Then move on to identify the focus of the question.
>
> In Question 1 this will be the extract and its links to your wider reading.
>
> In the poetry question, the focus of your essay will be:
>
> ■ **either** a **critical opinion** about a **named poem** and its relation to **other poems** in the collection
>
> ■ **or** a **critical opinion** about the collection in general.
>
> You could do this work alone, or by working in a group and sharing your ideas.
>
> When you have finished you should move on and check how far your ideas match the ones suggested below.

■ Key words, focus and strategies in the examination room

We will now go through the questions in turn and look at the focus and the key words of each question. Then we will look at strategies for answering the question.

Section A

Question 1 (the compulsory question)

The **focus** of this question is an extract from a **letter** written by Vera Brittain to her mother in December 1917 and printed in *Letters from a Lost Generation*, as well as the **connections** you can make to your wider reading.

The **key words** in the question are:

- *writer's thoughts and feelings*
- *ways expresses them*
- *compare to wider reading*
- *how typical*
- *subject matter and style.*

Your strategy in the examination room should be above all to read closely and to plan and organise effectively. Your success in the examination will depend on this. Here is our advice:

1 Take enough time to read the question very carefully, underlining or highlighting the key words.

2 **Read the extract very closely and consider what Vera Brittain is writing about (the subject matter)**, paying particular attention to her **thoughts and feelings.**

3 Then you should turn to a consideration of how she expresses those thoughts and feelings (**her style**).

4 When you have read the extract closely several times and have made detailed notes on it, you should start to consider what connections come to mind with your wider reading in the literature of World War One.

5 First think of similarities in your wider reading in the areas of:
- thoughts and feelings
- genre – a letter in this case
- writing style
- the gender of the writer
- time of writing.

6 Then turn to 'differences' in your wider reading, using the same categories.

7 These notes will help you to decide **how typical** the extract is of writing from or about World War One and will form the basis of your essay.

8 Remember that all four Assessment Objectives are tested in this question, so as you plan, and then as you write, you need to be sure that you:
- shape your ideas into a coherent, well-illustrated answer
- explore the ways Brittain and other writers use form, structure and language to shape meaning
- make connections between the Brittain extract and your wider reading
- trace the influence of the World War One context on Brittain's extract.

Section B

All the poetry questions target the same Assessment Objectives, and we will return to these after we have considered the focus and the key words of each question.

Link

Turn back to Chapter 1 and look at the advice we gave about close reading. Use those questions to support your close reading in this section.

Up the Line to Death: ed. Brian Gardner

Question 2

The **focus** of this question is **either 2 or 3** poems **or** a wide selection of poems.

The **key words** are:

- ■ *one mood*
- ■ *single focus*
- ■ *how far do you agree*.

Question 3

The **focus** of this question is the poem '**High Wood**' and the rest of the anthology.

The **key words** of the question are:

- ■ *how far do you agree*
- ■ *appropriate conclusion*.

Scars Upon My Heart: ed. Catherine Reilly

Question 4

The **focus** of this question is **either 2 or 3** poems **or** a wide range of poems.

The **key words** are:

- ■ *do not deal*
- ■ *realities of the war*
- ■ *how far do you agree*.

Question 5

The **focus** of this question is the poem '**Perhaps'**, and **other poems** in the collection.

The **key words** are:

- ■ *to what extent do you agree*
- ■ *this poem is the key*.

War Poetry: ed. Jon Stallworthy

Question 6

The **focus** of this question is **either 2 or 3** poems **or** a wide selection.

The **key words** are:

- ■ *how far do you agree*
- ■ *little variety*.

Question 7

The **focus** of this question is the poem '**MCMXIV**' and **other poems** in the selection.

The **key words** are:

■ *to what extent do you agree*

■ *this poem is the key.*

In Section B you have to answer **one** of these six questions. All these questions test the same three Assessment Objectives, so whichever question you answer, you should adopt the following strategy:

1 Read the question carefully, underlining or highlighting the **key words**.

2 **Look carefully at the critical opinion** in the question and choose the poems that will help you to construct the argument of your answer.

3 Remember that the question will ask **you how far or to what extent do you agree**, so you will need to consider both sides of the argument and find material to support your answer.

4 **Three Assessment Objectives** are assessed in this answer, so you need to ensure that:

■ you construct a well-argued, well-informed, coherent essay

■ you explore the ways the poet's choices of form, structure and language shape meaning

■ you compare and connect the poems in your text and explore interpretations of them.

■ Assessment

You may want to ask your teacher to assess your answers to the specimen questions, you may wish to assess your own work or to work in a group with your peers, looking at each other's work.

Here is a summary of the bands of achievement:

■ If your work has the features of Band 1 work – **inaccurate, irrelevant, assertive** – you will not be writing at the required standard for AS.

■ If your work is **narrative, descriptive and generalised** in its approach to the text, it will be assessed in Band 2 of the grid.

■ If you are starting to **explore and analyse** the texts and to present your argument in a **coherent** fashion, your work will be assessed in Band 3.

■ If your work is **coherent, cogent, mature, fluent and sophisticated**, it will be assessed in Band 4.

You can go on from here to make up your own questions and to practise selecting material, planning, organising and writing your responses. The purpose of this book, and of your whole AS English Literature course, has been to encourage you to develop as an **informed, independent reader**, and, if you have followed the advice and taken part in the activities, you can be confident that you will have achieved that, and that your success in the AS course is assured.

■ **Link**

However you choose to assess your work, you need to go back to Chapter 1 and remind yourself of the skills profiles of the different bands of achievement.

Glossary

A

anchorage: a fixing device – the text directs the reader through the signifiers of the image towards a meaning chosen in advance by the producer of the text.

Active creator: a maker of meaning; a reader who has individual ideas rather than re-cycling the ideas of others.

Active engagement: thinking for yourself about the text you are reading.

Adaptation: a modified literary text in a different genre to the original work; usually a novel or a play made into a film.

Analyse: *see* 'close reading'.

Assertive: *see* 'unsupported assertion'.

Assessment objectives: these identify the skills which candidates need to display in their examination answers.

Autobiography: a non-fiction text which presents a first person version of the writer's life.

B

Background: *see* 'context'.

Ballad: a simple narrative poem written in the third person.

Biographical notes: a short summary of a writer's life.

Biography: a non-fiction text which presents a third person version of the subject's life.

Brainstorm: gather together a range of relevant ideas before organising them into a coherent response.

C

Characters: the people in a novel, invented by the writer – they are not real people.

Chronological: telling the story in the order that the events occurred.

Close reading: focused, analytical reading which discovers multiple meanings through exploration of textual detail.

Cogent: convincing and persuasive; powerfully argued.

Coherent: well-organised; clear and well argued.

Combatant: a person who fights in a war, such as a soldier.

Comedy: a play with a happy ending, its main purpose is to make the audience laugh.

Context: the cultural, social and historical background to a literary text.

Context question: an examination question which requires the candidate to respond to an unprepared non-fiction prose extract and to place it in a wider literary and historical context.

Creative transformational writing: an imaginative response to a literary text which shows your knowledge and understanding through the ways in which you re-creation reflects the original text.

Critical opinion: a quotation from a literary critic, to which you should give balanced consideration in your poetry answer.

Cultural commentary: a non-fiction text which presents the writer's observations on a contemporary cultural, literary or artistic issue.

D

Descriptive: an answer which gives an account of the text rather than analysing the writer's techniques.

Diary: a first person account of events, not usually intended for publication.

Drama: *see* 'genre'.

Dramatic monologue: a narrative poem written in the first person.

E

Elegy: a reflective poem of mourning or loss.

Epic: a long narrative poem, often featuring heroic subject matter.

Essay: a short non-fiction text which treats its subject in a formal, systematic manner.

Explore: *see* 'close reading'.

Expressionism: a literary movement whose writers are noted for their presentation of emotion and inner feeling, rather than external reality.

F

Farce: comedy based on improbable events and exaggerated misunderstandings.

First person narrator: an author who writes in role as one of the characters in the story, using the first person (e.g. I, we) to present a perspective on events.

Fluent: written with impressive confidence and clarity.

Focus: the specific aspect of a literary text which you will write about in your coursework.

Frame narrator: a first person narrator whose story includes a second narrative related by a different character.

G

Gender: sex – either male or female.

Generalised: an answer which is broadly accurate but fails to consider the detail of the text.

Genre: the type of a literary text. The three main literary genres are prose, poetry and drama. These genres can be sub-divided: for instance, prose can be classified as fiction or non-fiction – and, in turn, fiction can be split into sub-genres such as the Gothic novel and the Bildungsroman.

Gothic: a branch of Romanticism concerned with the sinister and the supernatural. The genre includes horror novels such as Mary Shelley's *Frankenstein*.

H

How typical: in what ways is the extract similar to, or different from, other writing of the same historical period?

I

Imaginative re-construction: *see* 'creative transformational writing'.

Inaccurate: an answer containing errors.

Independent: *see* 'active creator'.

Informed response: a response based on knowledge and understanding.

Inter-textuality: the establishment of links and connections between different literary texts.

Interview: A spoken word forms which, in transcript, constitutes a non-fiction text.

Introduction: an integral, informative opening section of a text.

Irrelevant: an answer that has nothing to do with the question that was asked.

K

Key words: the most important words in an examination question: the ones you must address in your answer.

L

Literary criticism: a non-fiction text which analyses literature in an academic manner.

Literature in translation: texts that were originally written in a language other than English.

Lyric poem: a short, song-like poem.

M

Maker of meaning: *see* 'active creator'.

Marking grid: a tool which enables examiners to measure candidates' abilities according to the Assessment Objectives and then award the appropriate marks.

Mature: fully developed; displaying a mastery of the text.

Melodrama: an exaggerated form of drama based on simple characters, excessive emotions and over-acting.

Memoir: a first person account of events, usually intended for publication.

Multiple narrators: the author tells the story through several different first person narrators.

N

Named poem: some examination questions name a specific poem as the subject for debate. You will also need to link it to other poems in your answer.

Narrative: the story and the way it is told.

Non-chronological: mixing up the order of events to create narrative effects.

Non-combatant: a person who doesn't fight, a civilian.

O

Omniscient/third person narrator: an author who knows everything the characters are thinking and uses the third person (e.g. he, she, they) to reveal the characters' thoughts and feelings to the reader.

Open letter: a published letter which any member of the reading public can access.

P

Pastiche: a text which imitates the work of another writer.

Personal informed interpretation: a coursework response with a focus on what you find interesting about a particular aspect of the text.

Personal response: a response which features your own relevant ideas about a text.

Plot: the things that happen in a novel.

Poetry: *see* 'genre'.

Preface: a piece of writing at the beginning of a text which is not integral to the text itself.

Prescribed content: specific ideas, characters or quotations which are guaranteed to earn a candidate marks in the examination. (There is no prescribed content for this paper: the mark is determined by the overall quality of a candidate's response.)

Prose: *see* 'genre'.

R

Realism: the presentation of life as it really is, rather than in a romantic or glamorous way.

Romanticism: a revolutionary literary movement of the late eighteenth and early nineteenth centuries. Romantic writers are noted for their celebration of the individual imagination and their spiritual approach to nature.

S

Satire: a humorous play which mocks or questions contemporary values.

Setting: the places in which the events of a novel occur.

Shared context: the background common to a collection of texts from the same historical period.

Skimpy: thin, superficial, underdeveloped.

Social drama: a play presenting the state of contemporary society (*see also* Social realism).

Social realism: the presentation of society and everyday life as they really are.

Sonnet: a fourteen-line poem.

Sophisticated: subtle and skilful; not afraid to tackle the complexities of the text; reading at a very high level.

Speech: a spoken word form which, in transcript, constitutes a non-fiction text.

Stream of consciousness: a modern literary technique which presents the reader with a character's uninterrupted thoughts.

Structure: the ways in which the distinctive features of a text, such as its narrative or its chronology, are organised.

Style: the writer's choices of language, form and structure – and the effects created by these choices.

T

Thematically: grouped and arranged according to theme or subject matter.

Travelogue: a first person account of the writer's travels.

Trilogy: a sequence of three novels, often featuring the same characters.

Typicality: the ways in which a text is characteristic of the writing of a particular historical period.

U

Unsupported assertion: a claim that is not backed up by any evidence from the text.

Utopia: a perfect society.

W

Wide reading: reading a range of different texts, in all three literary genres, within the shared context. A list of suggested wide reading texts is contained in Chapter One.

Index